Through My Lens: People, Places & Things
By Patti Schwartz

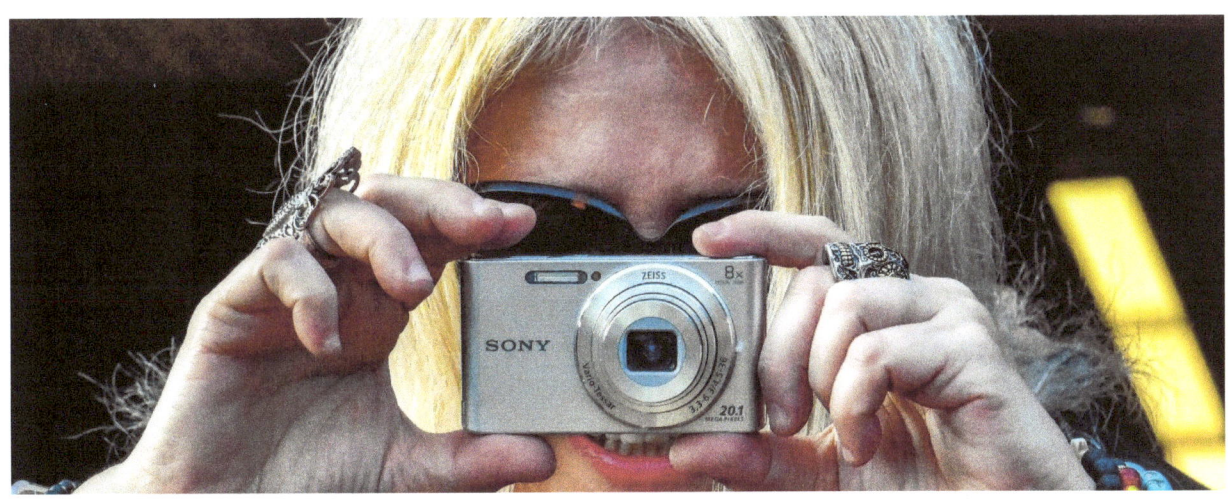

Introduction	**3**
The Conversation	3
The Evolution of the Image	3
The People	**5**
Politicians	5
The Performers	11
The Characters	18
The Children	26
The Athletes	29
Event Favorites	36
Places	**39**
Local	39
Alexandria Bay (Thousand Islands), NY	42
New York City	46
Cape Canaveral, Florida	49
Nassau, The Bahamas	52
The Finger Lakes	55
Things	**60**
Unusual and Unexpected	60
Furry, Feathery & In Between	66
Floral Beauty	75
Conclusion	**79**

Introduction

A decade ago, my life was in shambles through no one's fault but my own. Bad decisions were made and trust among family, friends, coworkers and community was broken. There was a period of time that I wallowed in my own self pity. I was lost. I felt I no longer had a purpose in life. That all changed with one conversation, much trial and error, and a camera.

The Conversation

After close to three years of working on repairing the family dynamic and self imposed social isolation, I bit the bullet and began to venture out into the community. It was not easy by any means and, at first, I was met with scorn and ridicule. It's true what they say. It's times of difficulty that show you who your true friends are.

It is also during times of difficulty that you meet someone who unwittingly changes your life for the better. It was a chance conversation with a virtual stranger that changed the direction of my life.

It was an innocent discussion centered around the events in and around our community that didn't seem to be getting the attention or the attendance they deserved. It was from this conversation that Patti Loves Bing was born.

The Evolution of the Image

Initially, it began with blog posts followed by admittedly grainy and blurry cell phone images. Over the course of the past six and a half years, I took it upon myself to learn everything I could about photography and eventually worked my way up from relying solely on my cell phone to a basic point and shoot camera until I finally felt comfortable enough in using a DSLR camera. My primary focus was to capture the memories of a community. A way to give back to all those in that community who never gave up on me.

As time went by, I became obsessed with capturing moments wherever I went; the people, places and things. That is why I felt the urge to write this book. To highlight some of my favorite images captured not only locally; but also throughout my travels.

The People

Capturing both candid and posed photos of everyday people enjoying themselves has become one of my favorite things to do with a camera. There have also been moments when I was able to get shots of some very well known people.

Politicians

Notwithstanding political views, it was personally satisfying to be able to capture the following memories of some national and regional politicians.

When former President Bill Clinton visited our area to campaign for his wife, Hilary, it was an honor to have been invited to join the press pool. Not many people can say that they were in the same room with a former president of the United States.

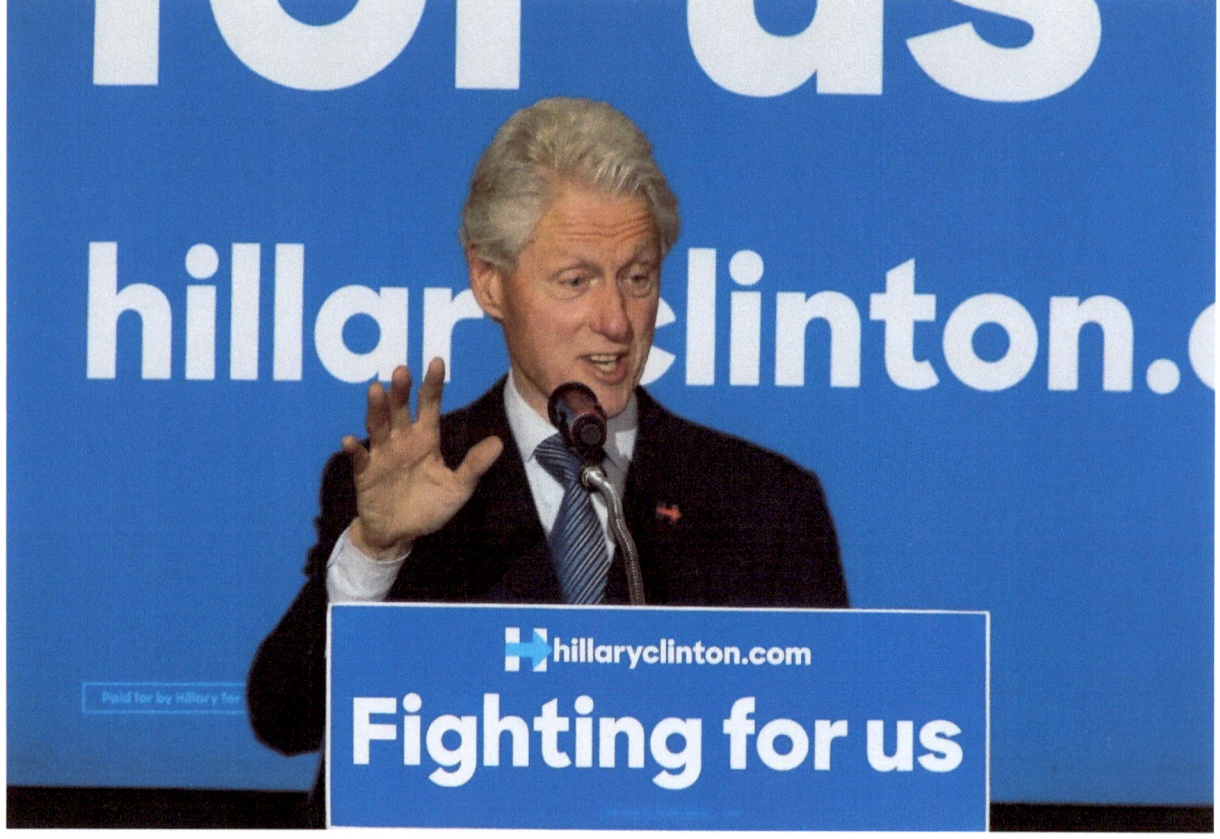

Regional and local politicians did not escape my lens. Actually, there are more than these examples of a few of my favorites.

New York State Governor Andrew Cuomo and New York City Mayor Bill DiBlasio celebrating World Pride Day this past June in New York City.

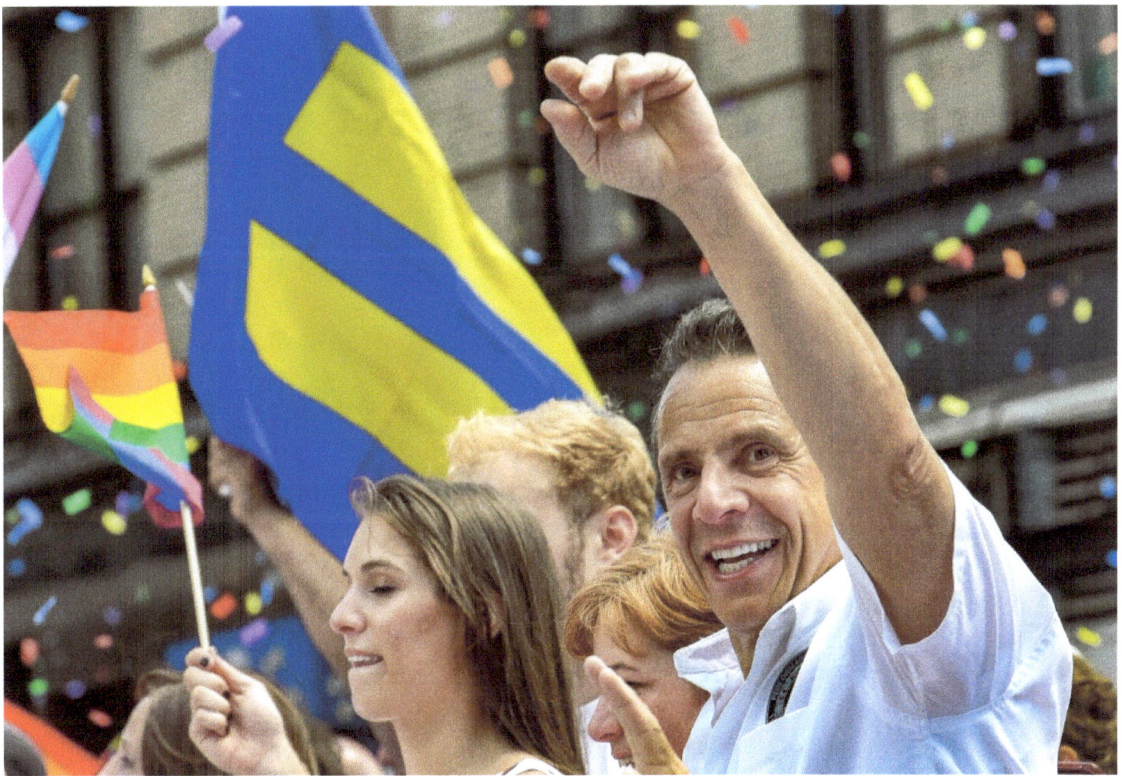

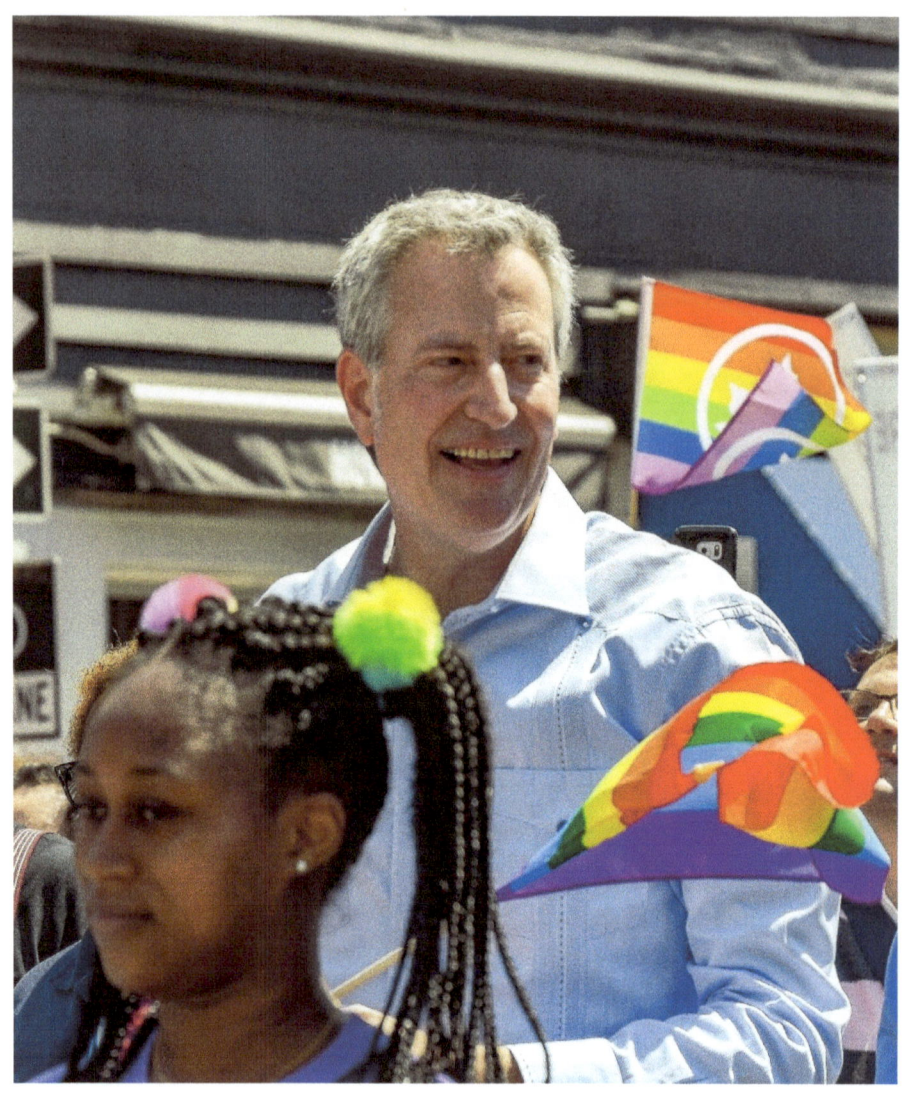

United States Congressman Anthony Brindisi and US Senator Chuck Schumer could always be counted on to make appearances at many of our local events. Senator Schumer, in particular, with his trusted bullhorn.

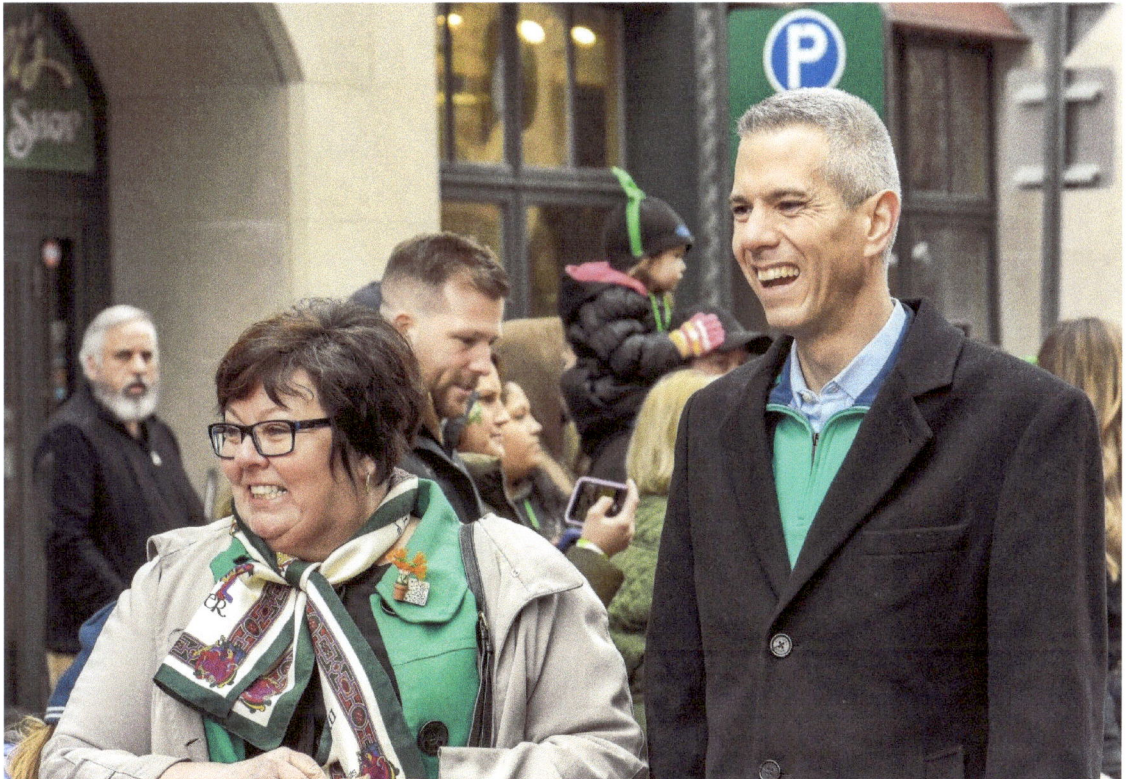

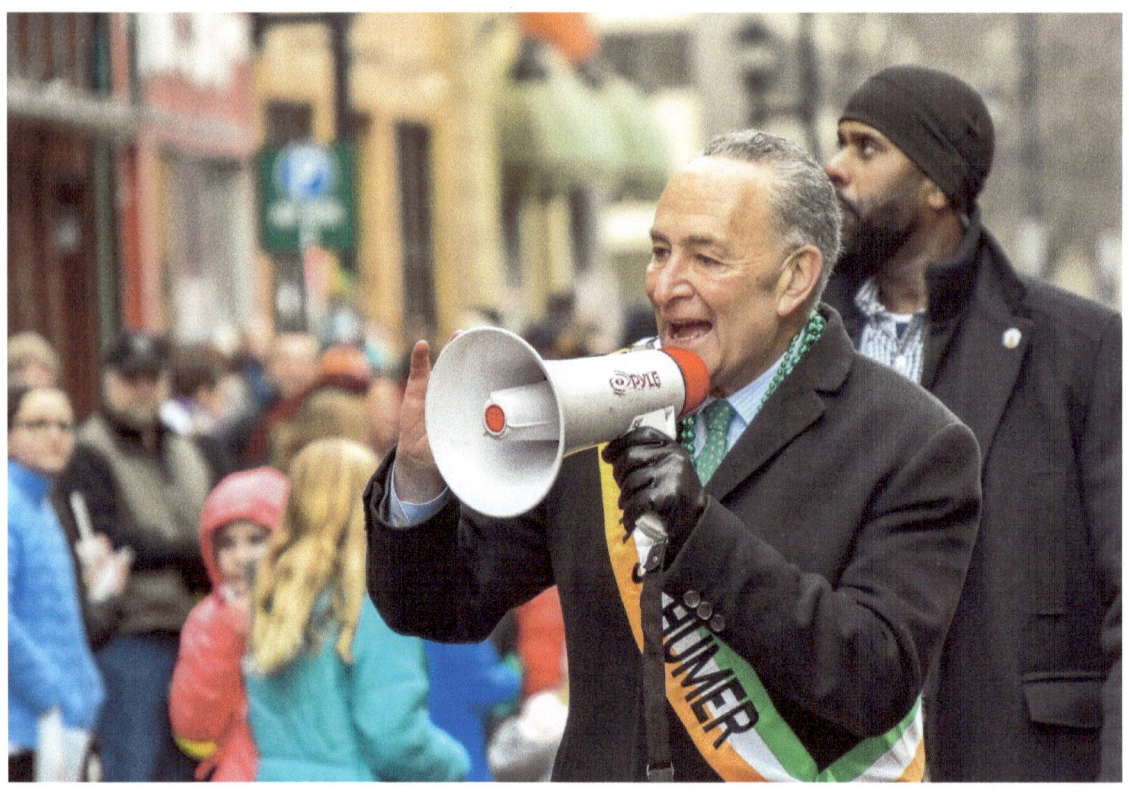

The Performers

Whether it be rocking it out on stage before an overly enthusiastic crowd or taking on a role in a play or a musical, capturing performers enjoying themselves as much as their fans has its own rewards.

One of my first images of said performers was this unplanned encounter of former American Idol contestants enjoying a stroll together through our small Upstate New York city.

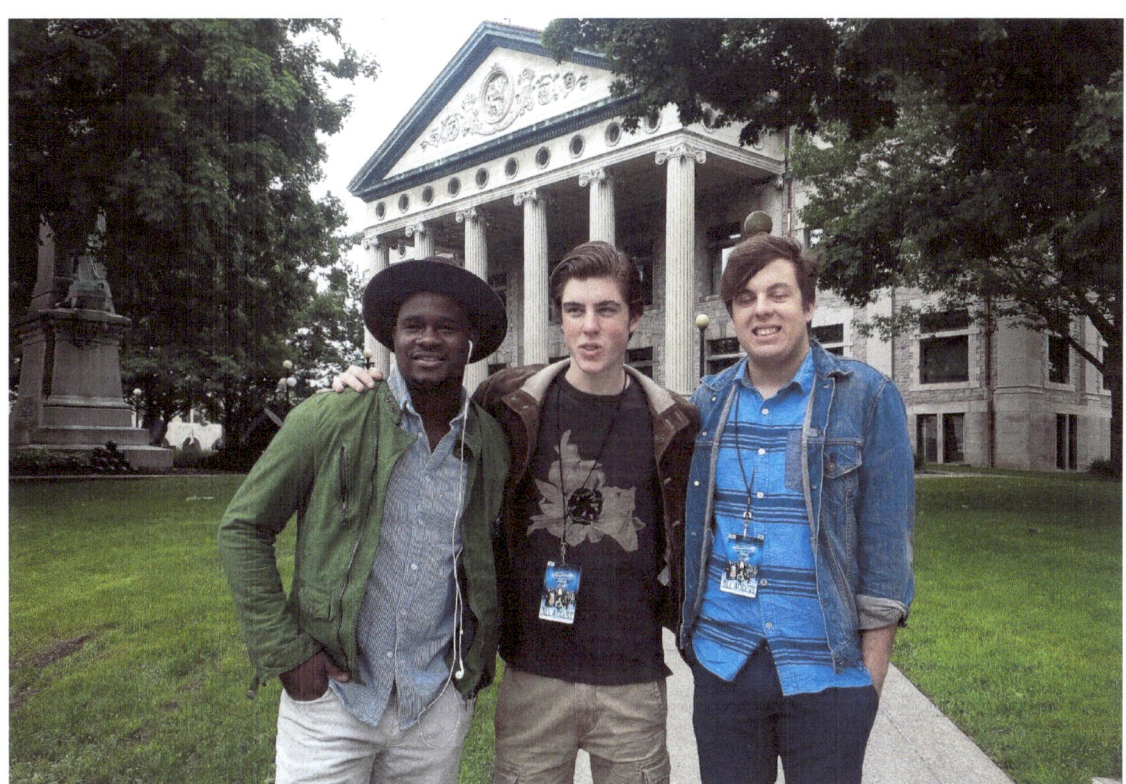

Grabbing the following shots of some nationally known musicians provided both personal and professional memories. It is not surprising that some of my personal favorites of Rick Springfield, Joan Jett & the Blackhawks, America and K.C. & the Sunshine Band represent just a few of those musicians and bands that helped to shape my lifelong love of music.

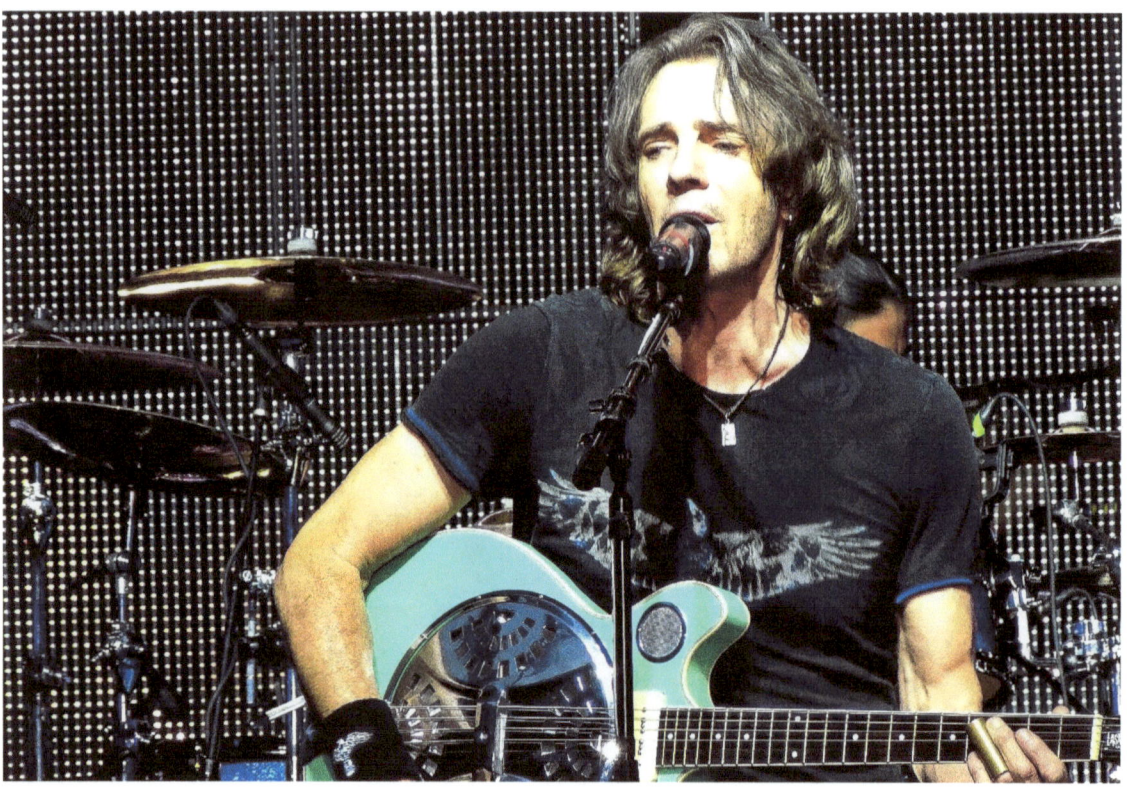

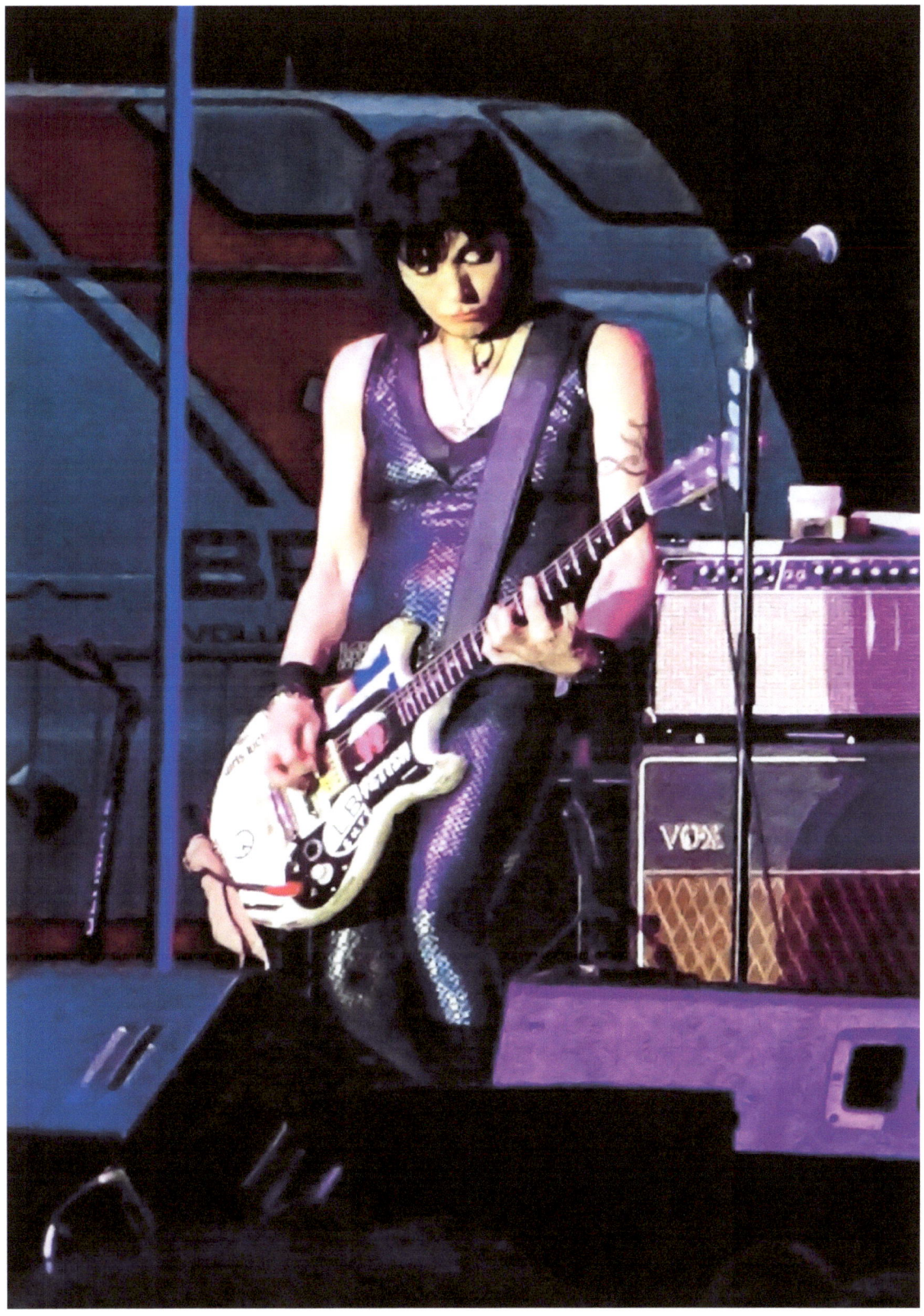

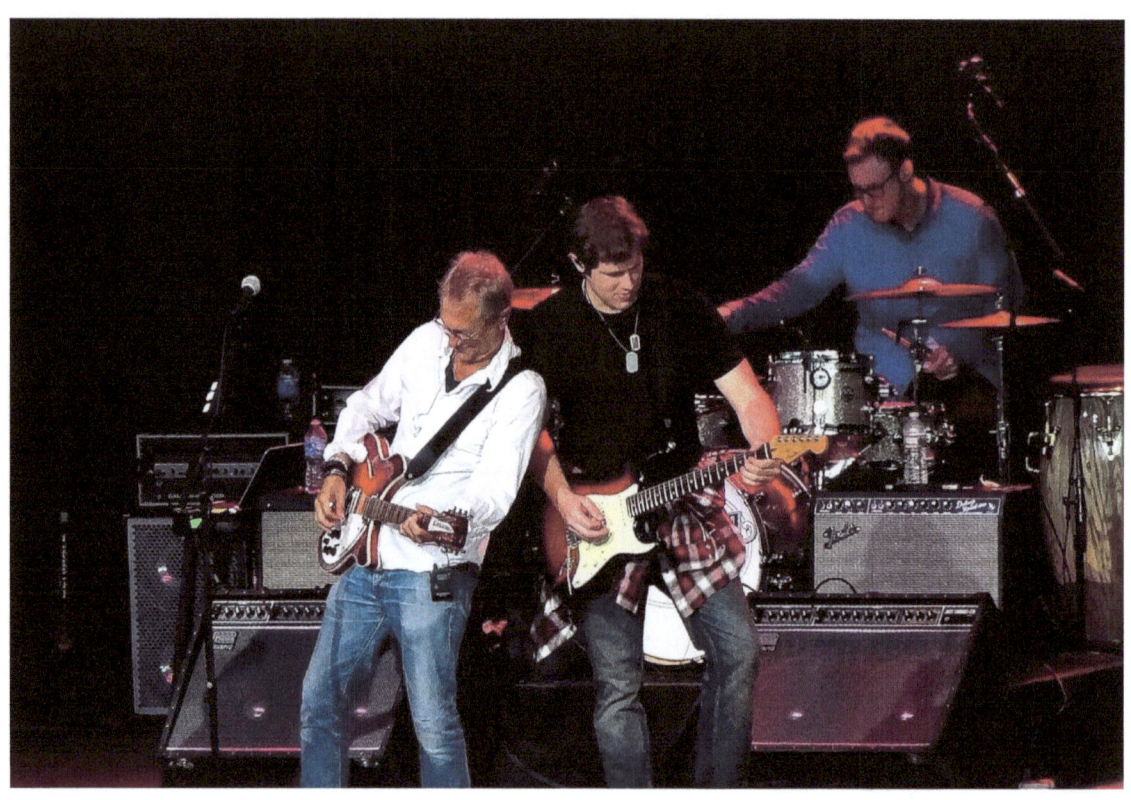

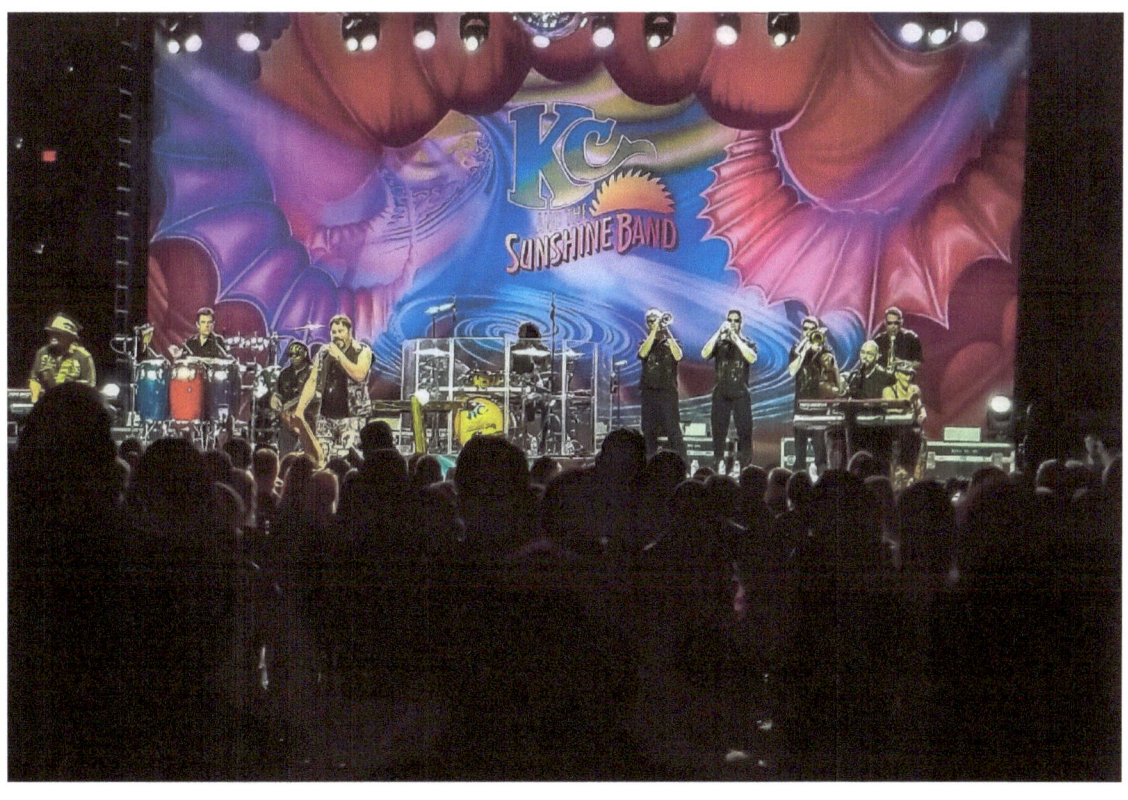

Nationally known musicians did not make up my entire collection of favorite performer photos. Locally here in the Southern Tier of New York, we are blessed to have extremely talented performers from all genres covering the wide spectrum of dance, comedy, opera, dramatic plays and musicals. A couple of my favorites follow but they should not be construed as a full representation of the talent that can be found in our little corner of the world.

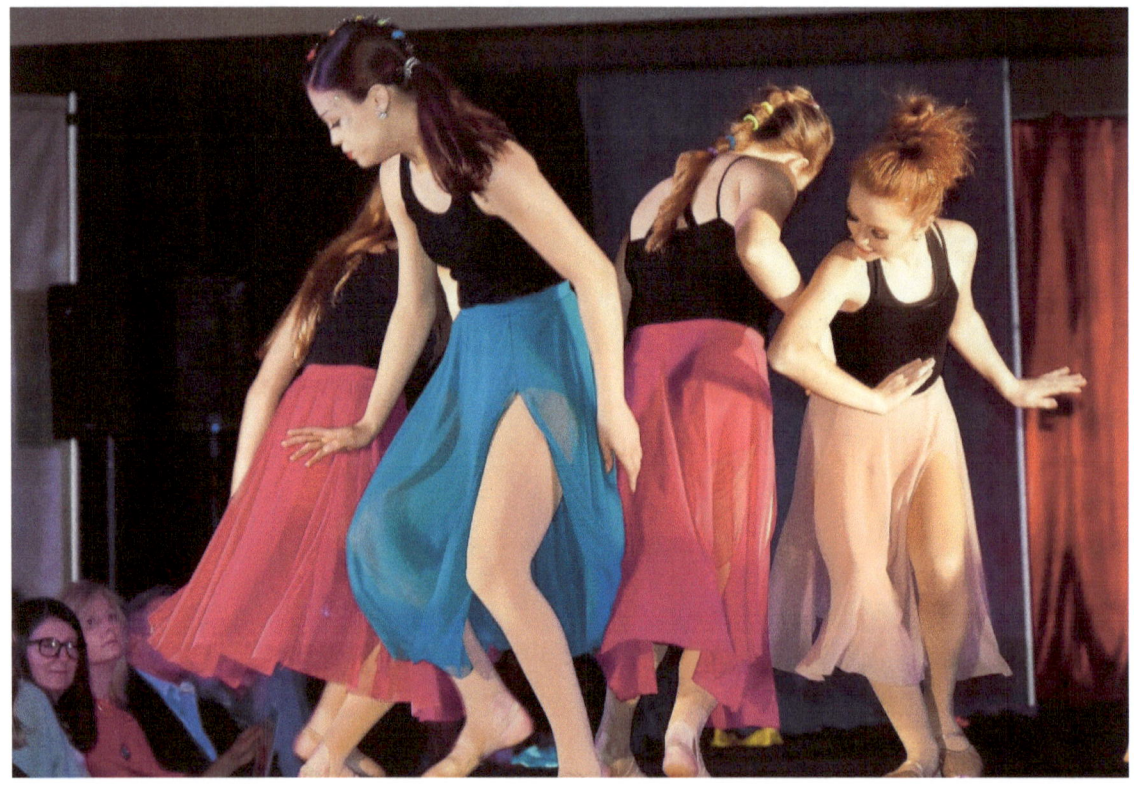

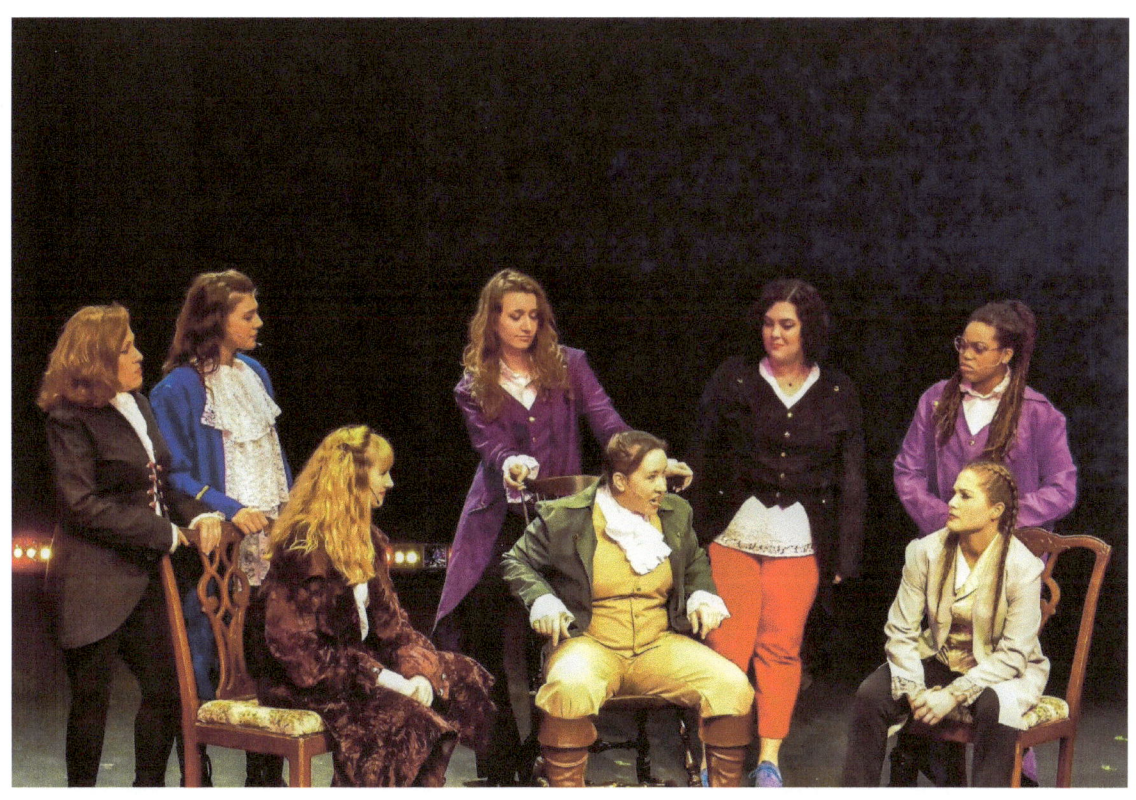

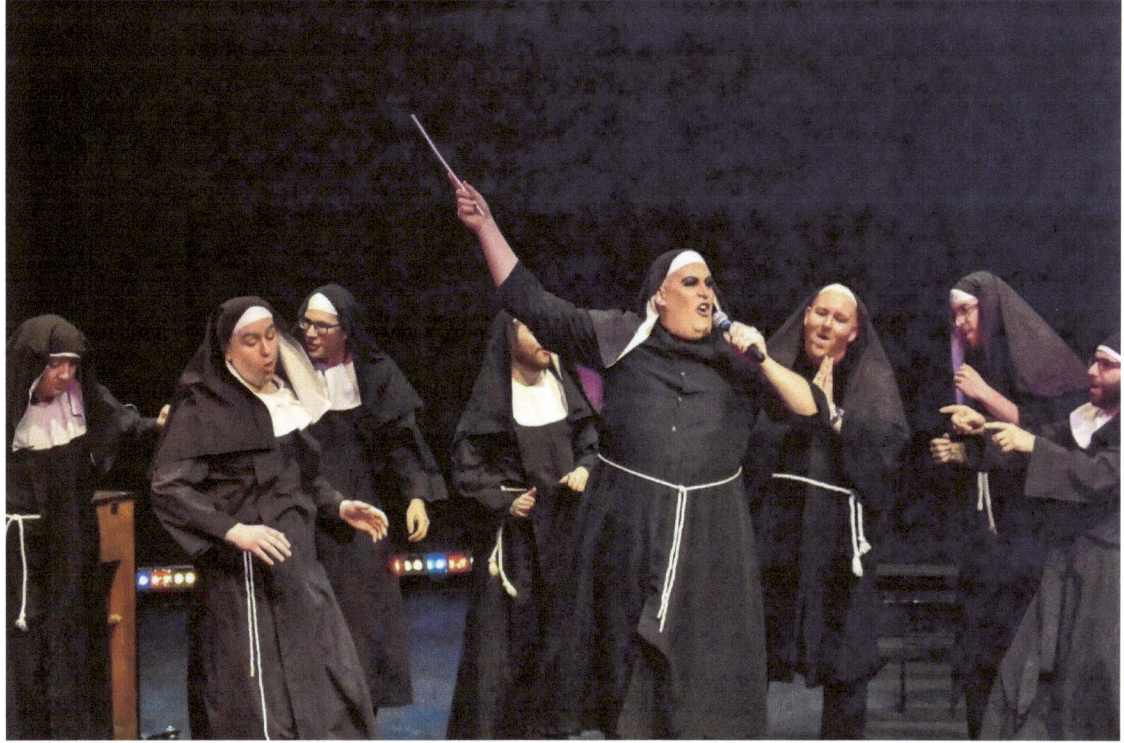

The Characters

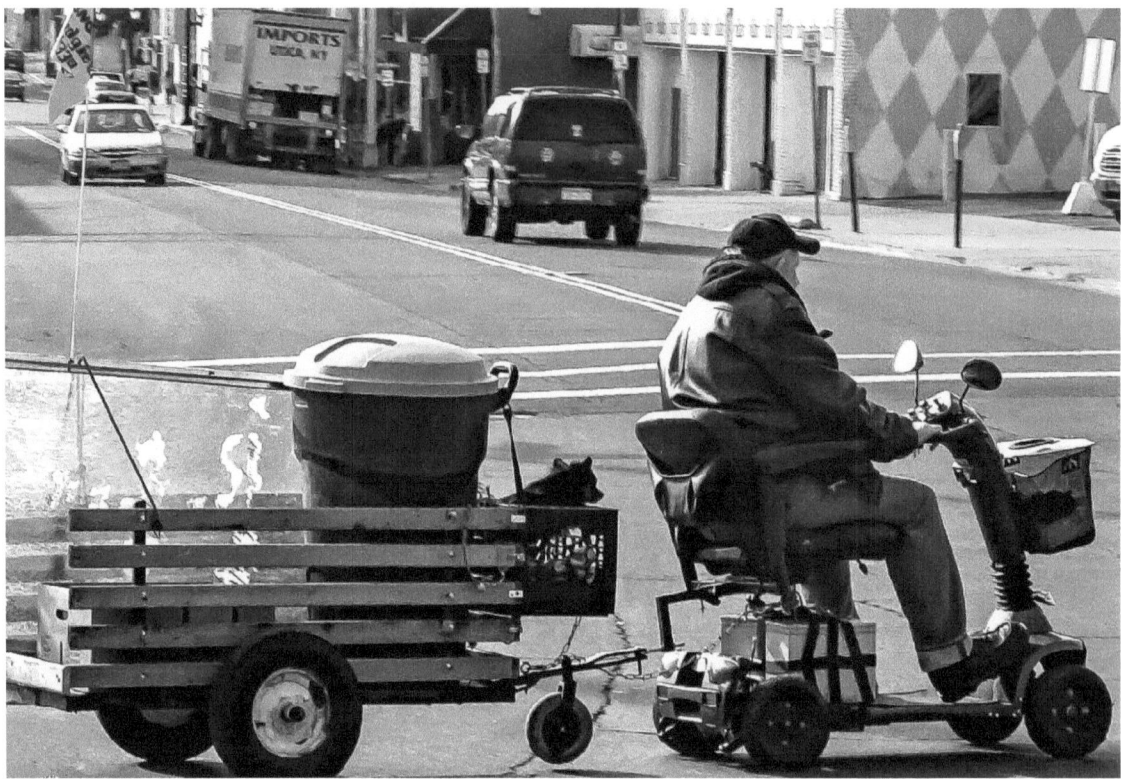

Encountering the unusual, eclectic and unexpected over the past several years has brought many thought provoking moments to my life as a photographer. You begin to wonder about the backstories; is it a cry for attention, their way of life or a very simply a way to bring a smile to those that they encounter? No matter what the reason, I consider myself lucky to have encountered each and every one of my "characters".

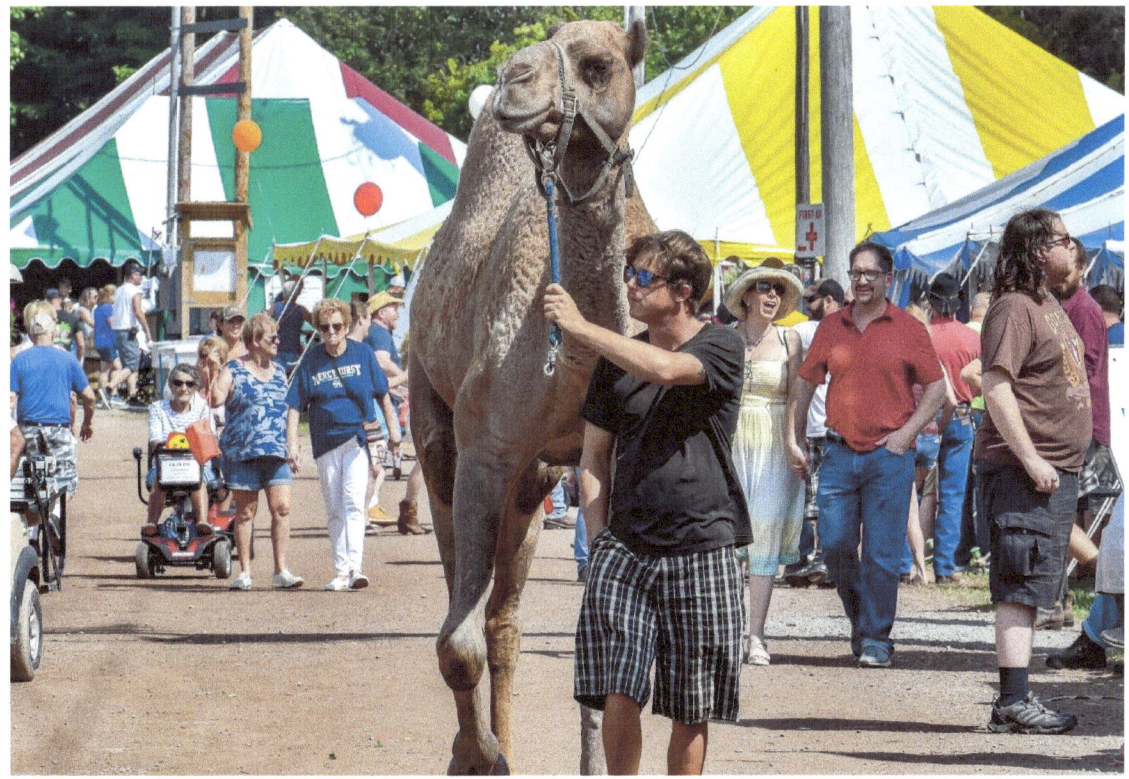

Out for a stroll with his camel during a local county fair didn't seem to turn many heads other than mine. It was as if this was a common occurrence.

However, some of the most interesting characters encountered over the past several years were those I was destined to capture as part of an event I was attending and photographing. There have been so many that to share them all would cover an entire publication on their own. It has been difficult to limit myself to just a few of my favorites.

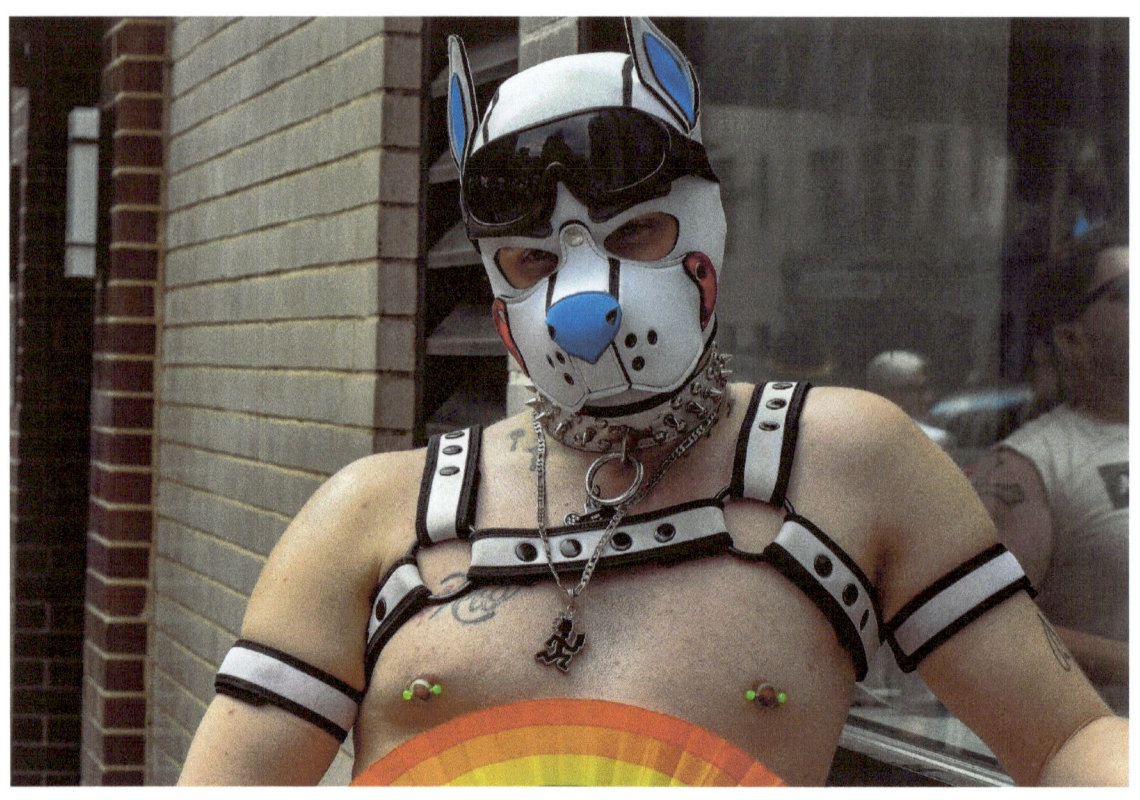

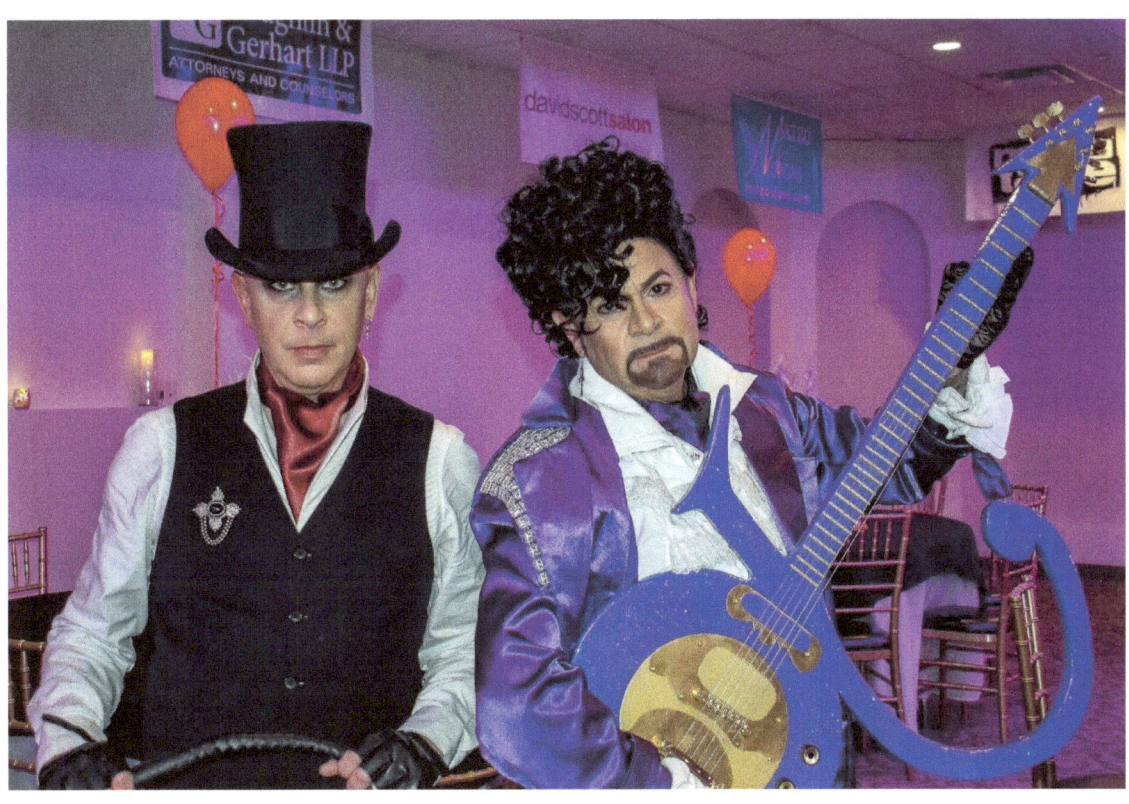

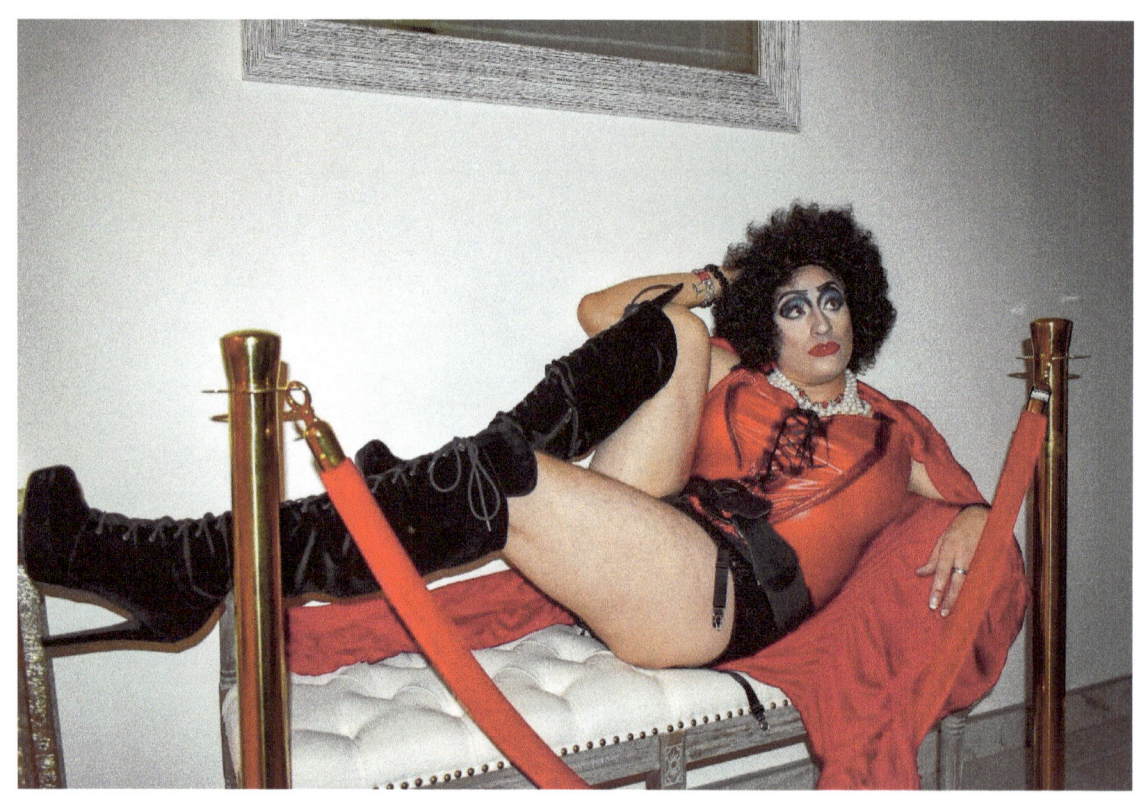

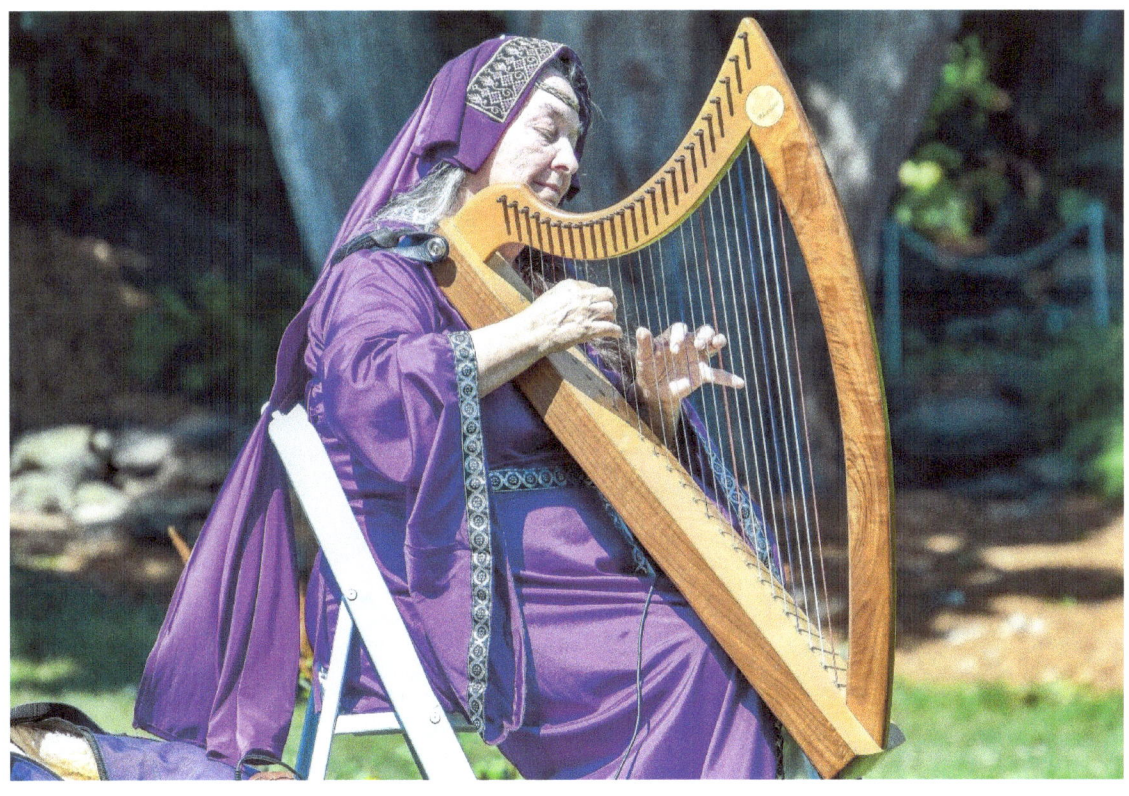

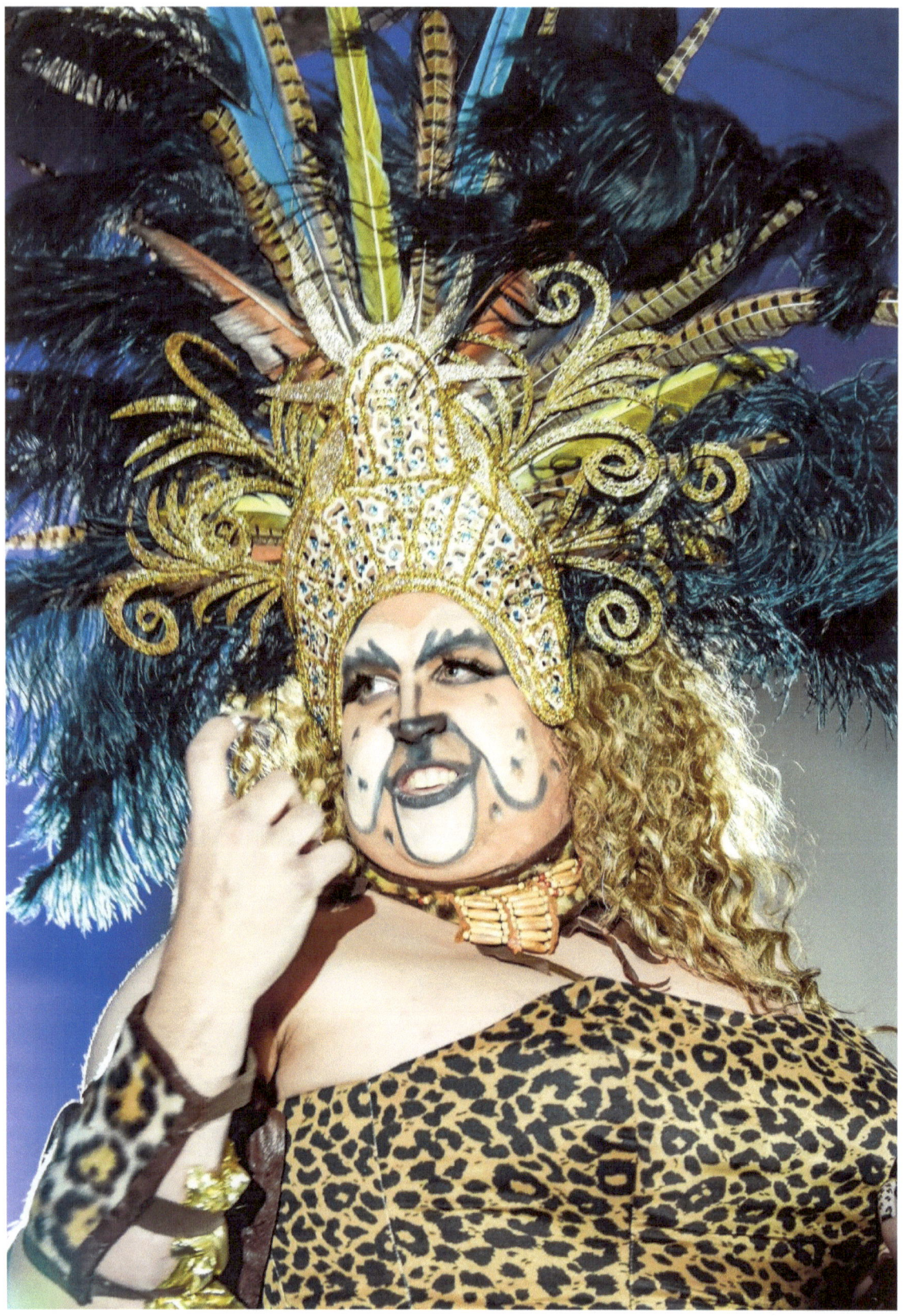

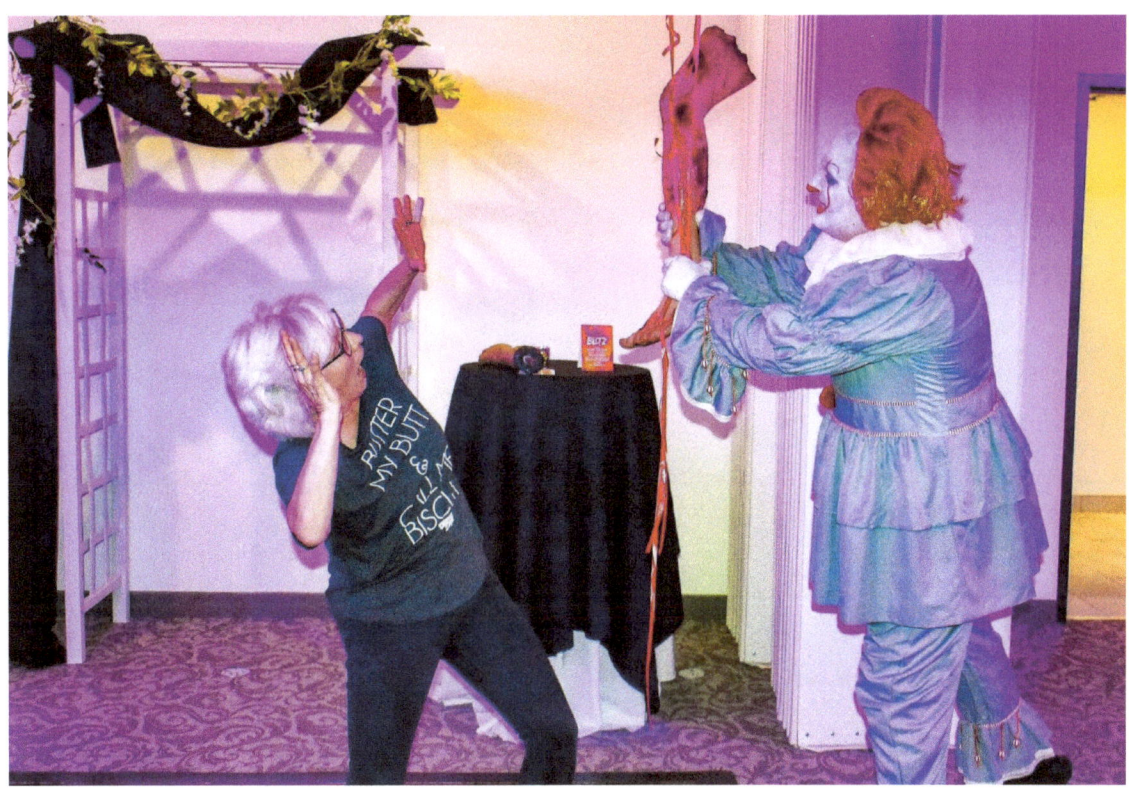

The Children

Throughout the years, the most memorable photos have been of the children. They represent the joy and innocence that so many of us have forgotten.

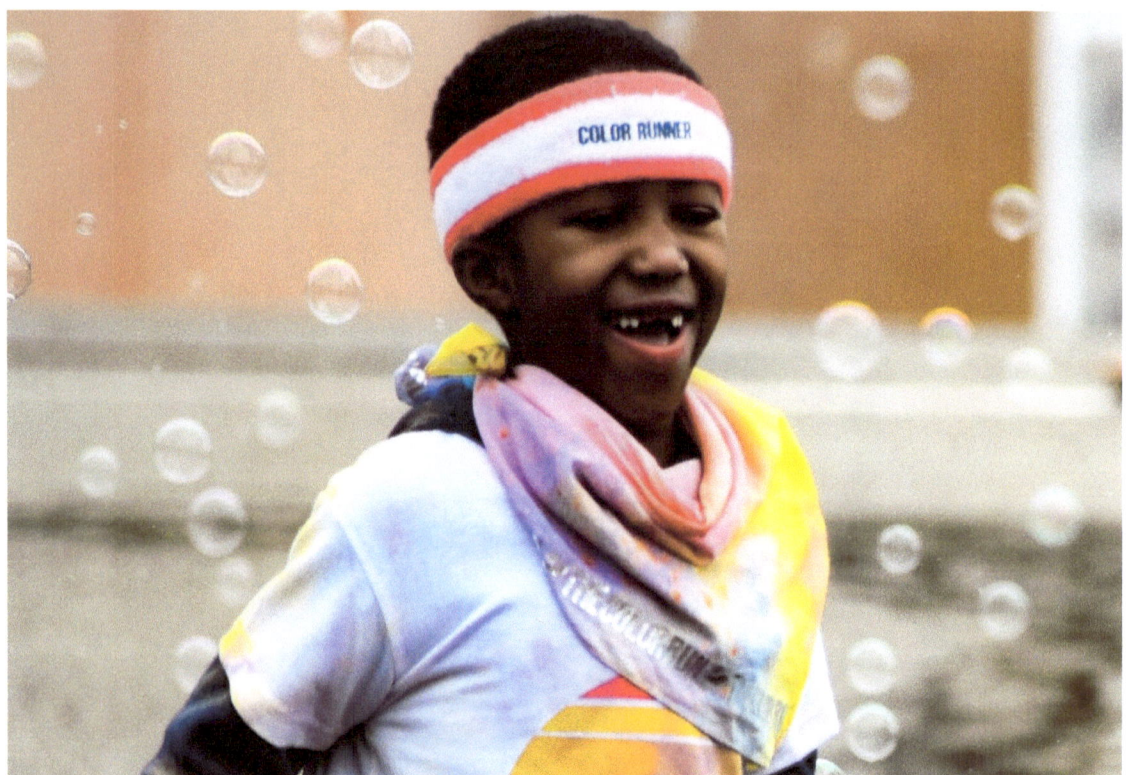

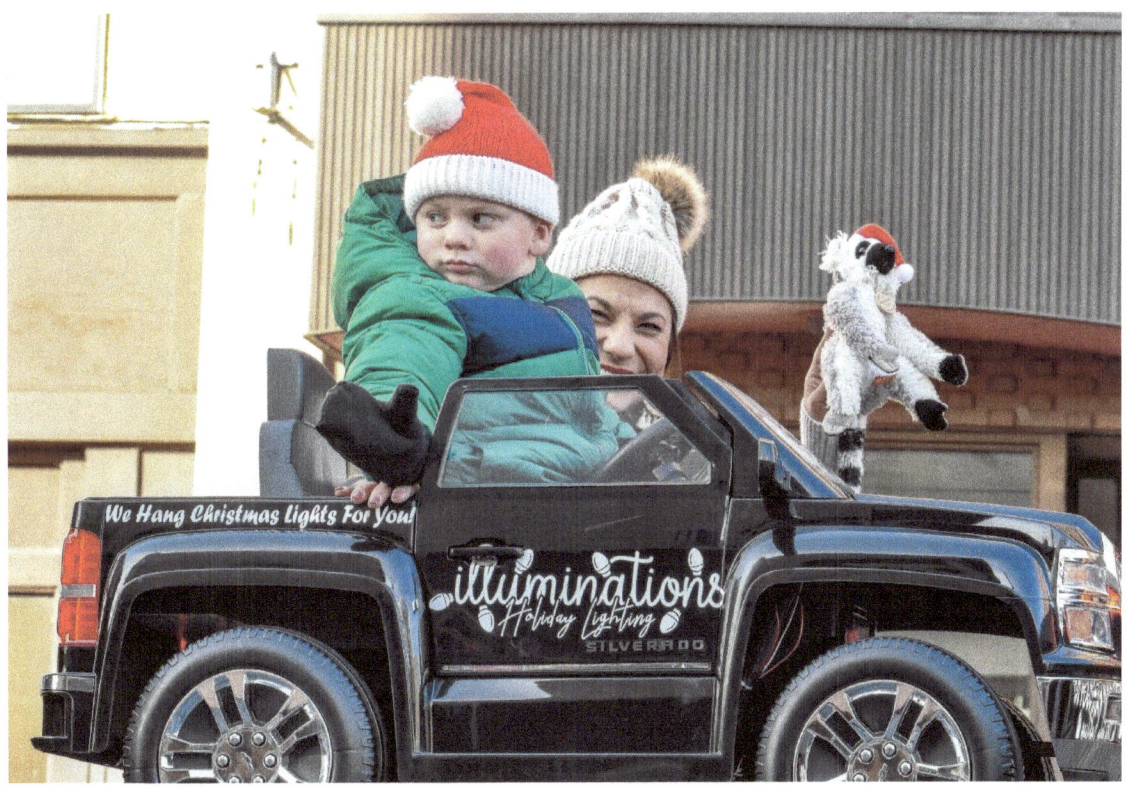
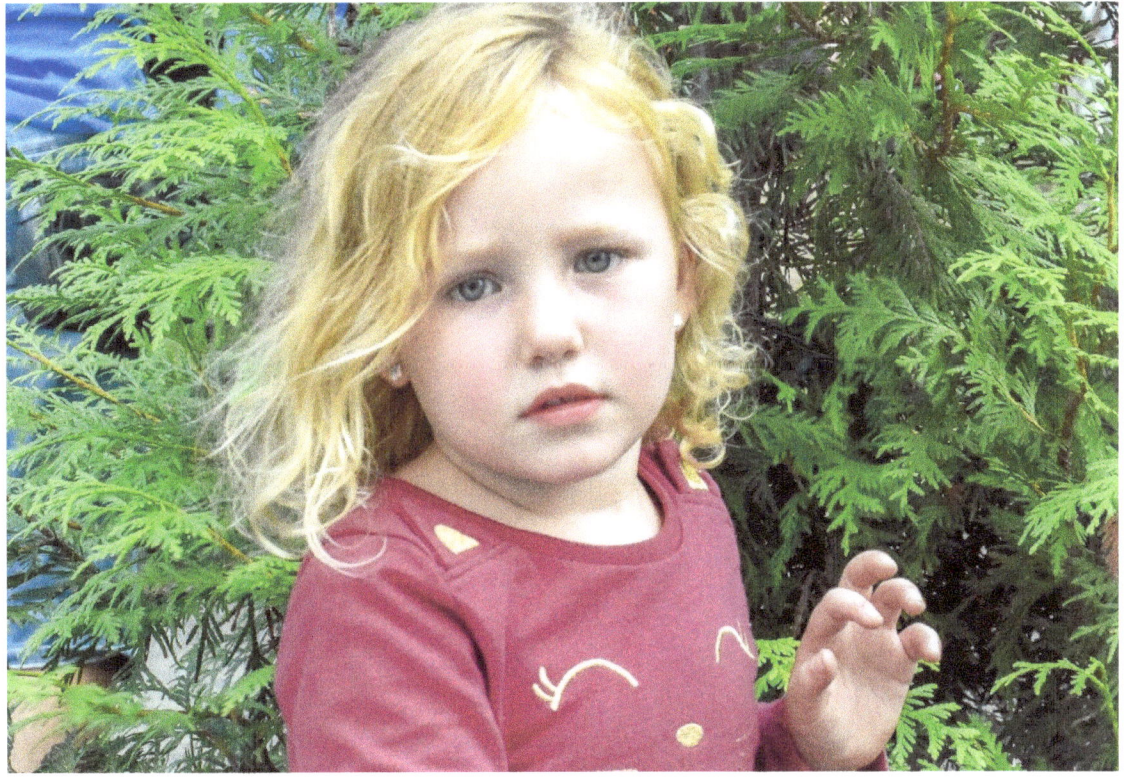

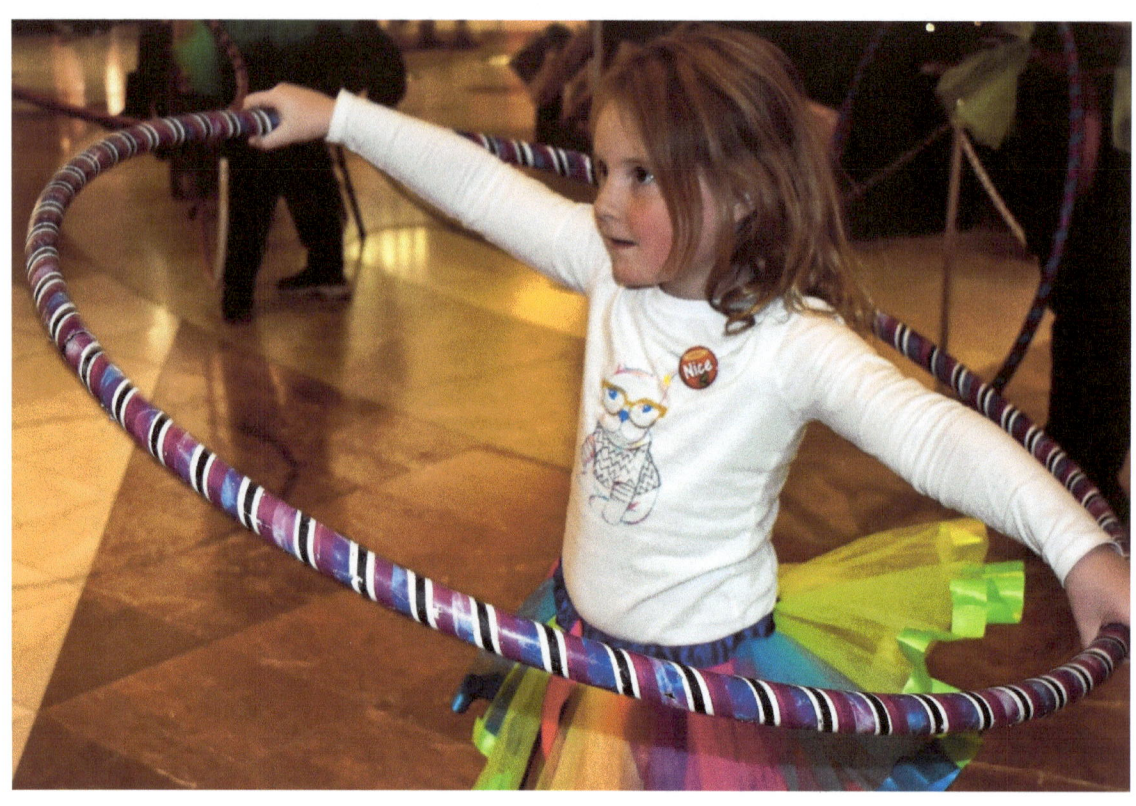

The Athletes

A collection of my favorite images would not be complete without including some of our local and regional runners and bikers. The stamina and motivation each of these athletes exude is beyond description and they all do it with huge smiles on their faces.

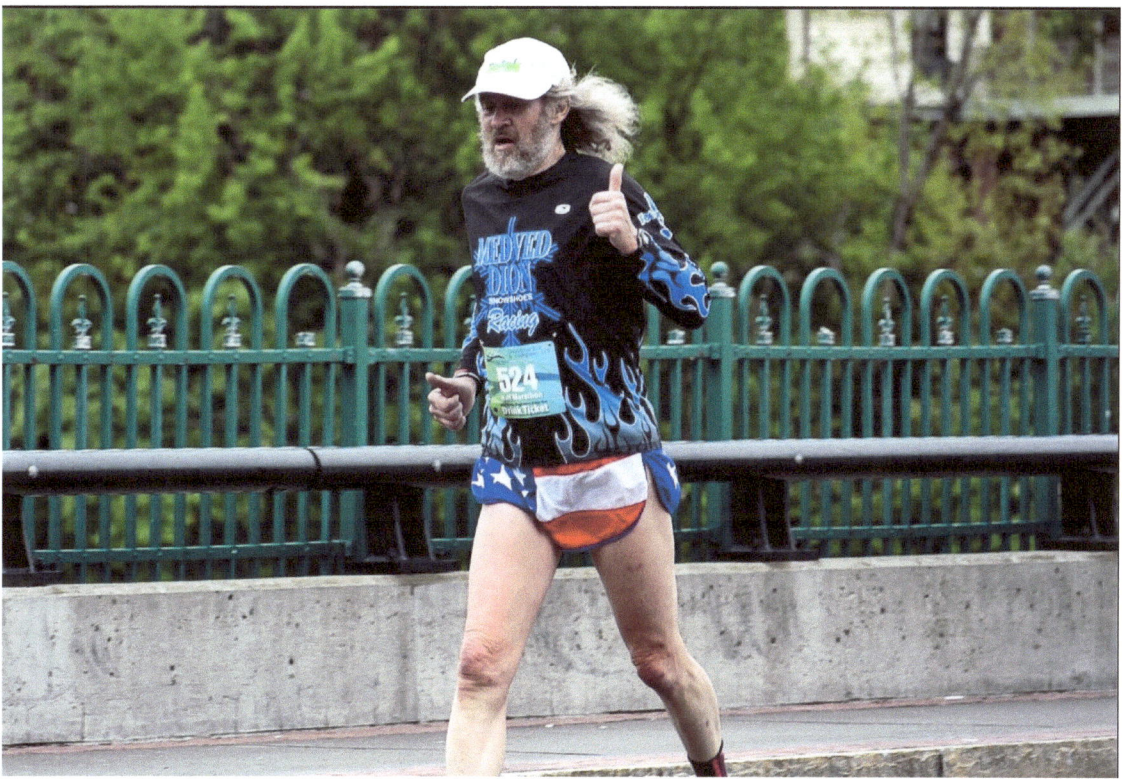

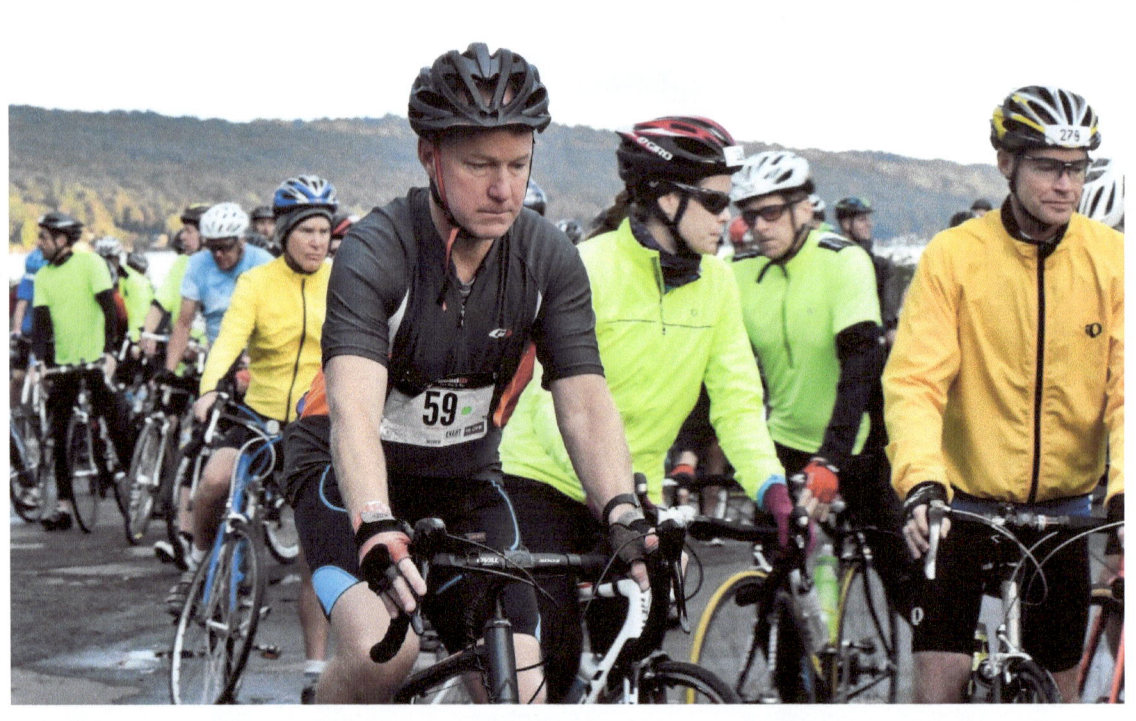

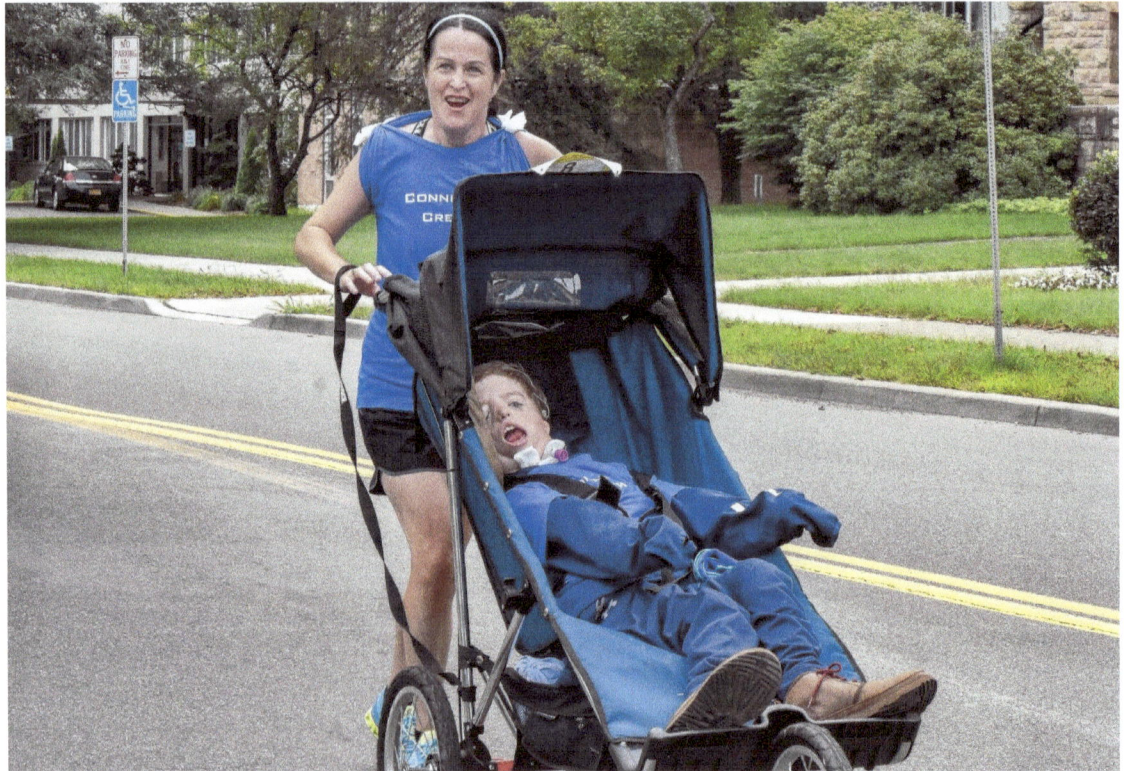

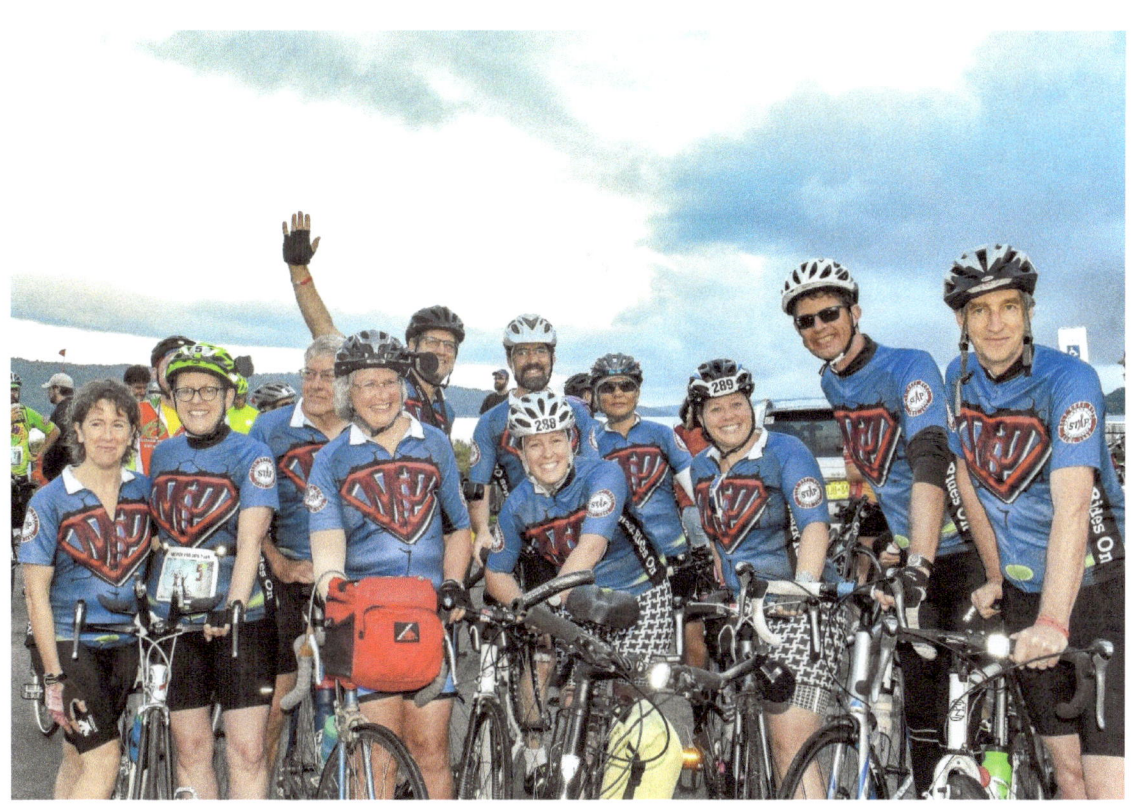

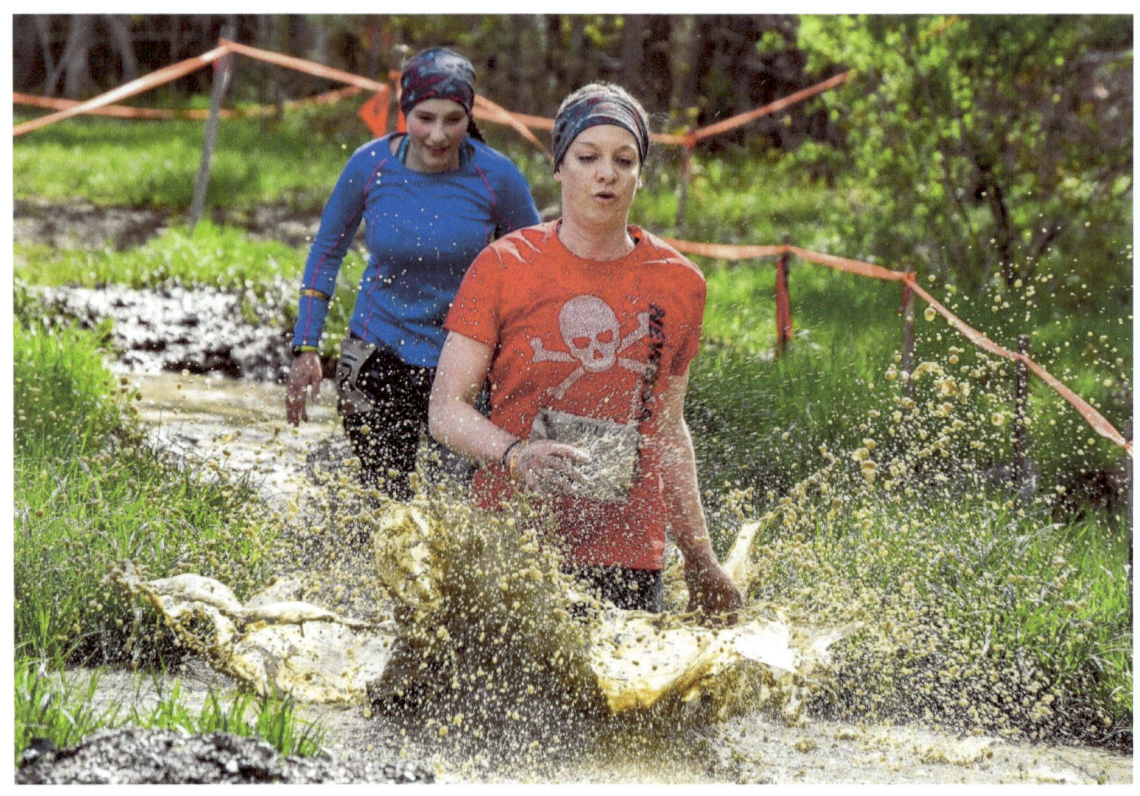
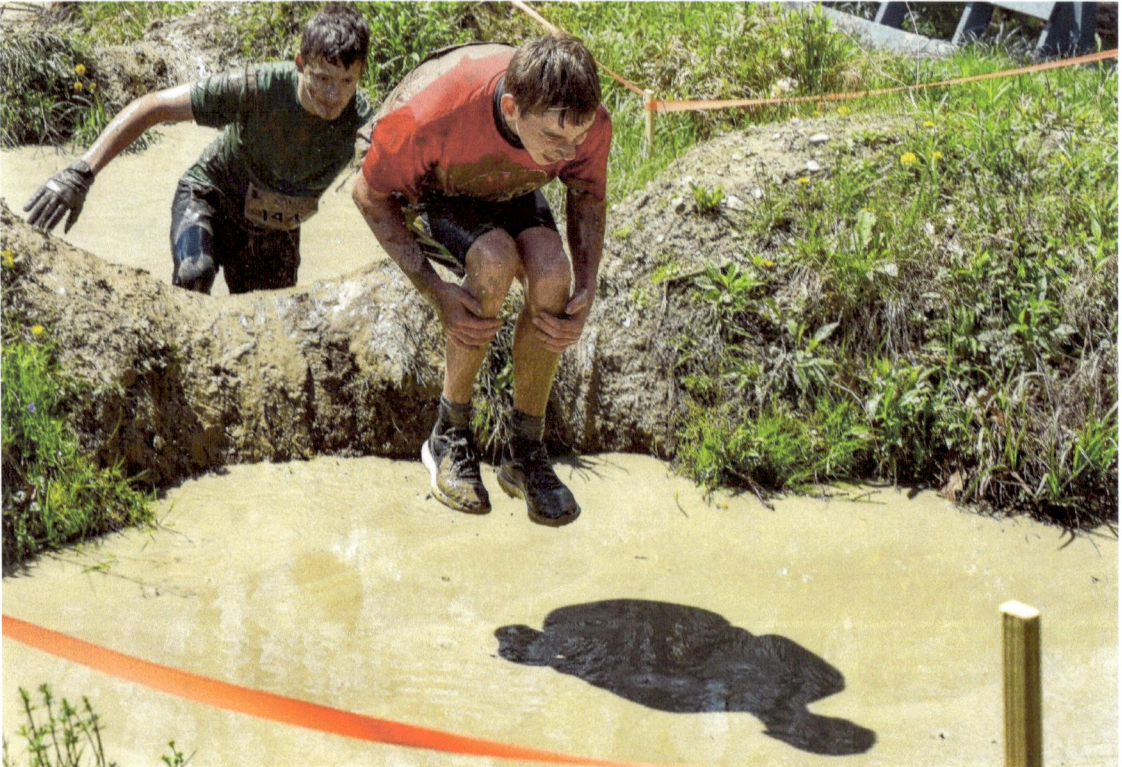

Of course, there are those athletes that exceeded in their campy take on the event they were competing in whether it be their costume of choice or simply their attitude.

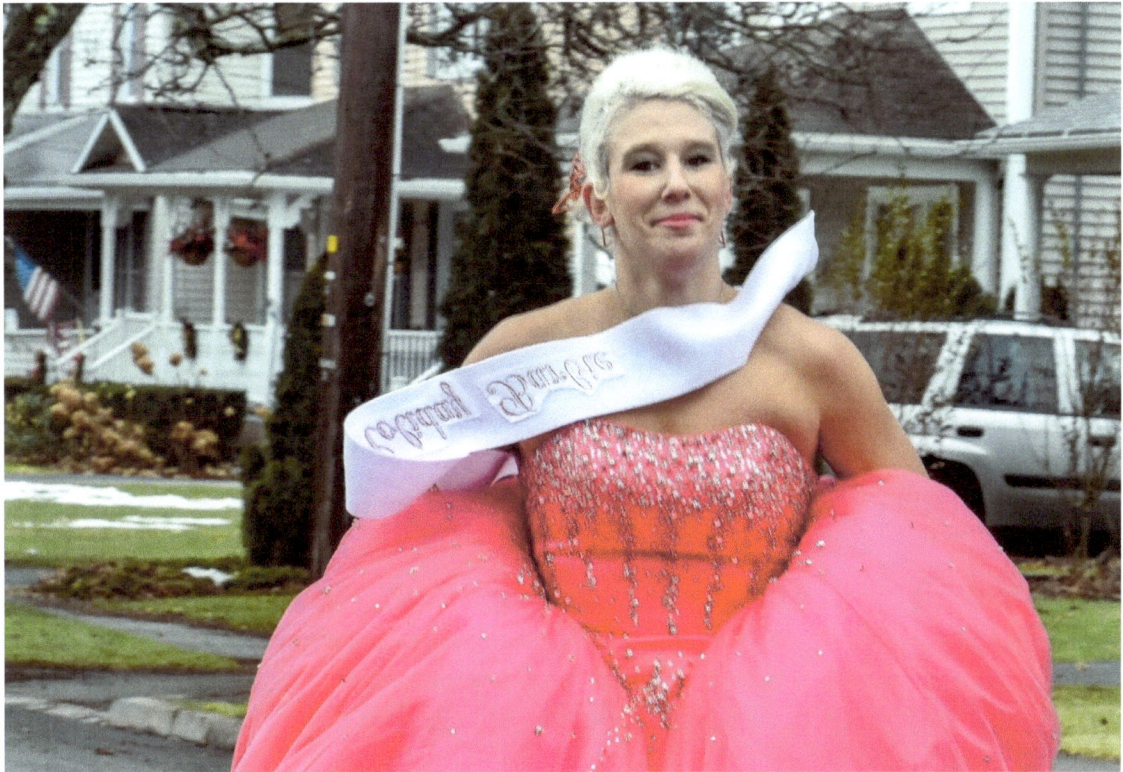

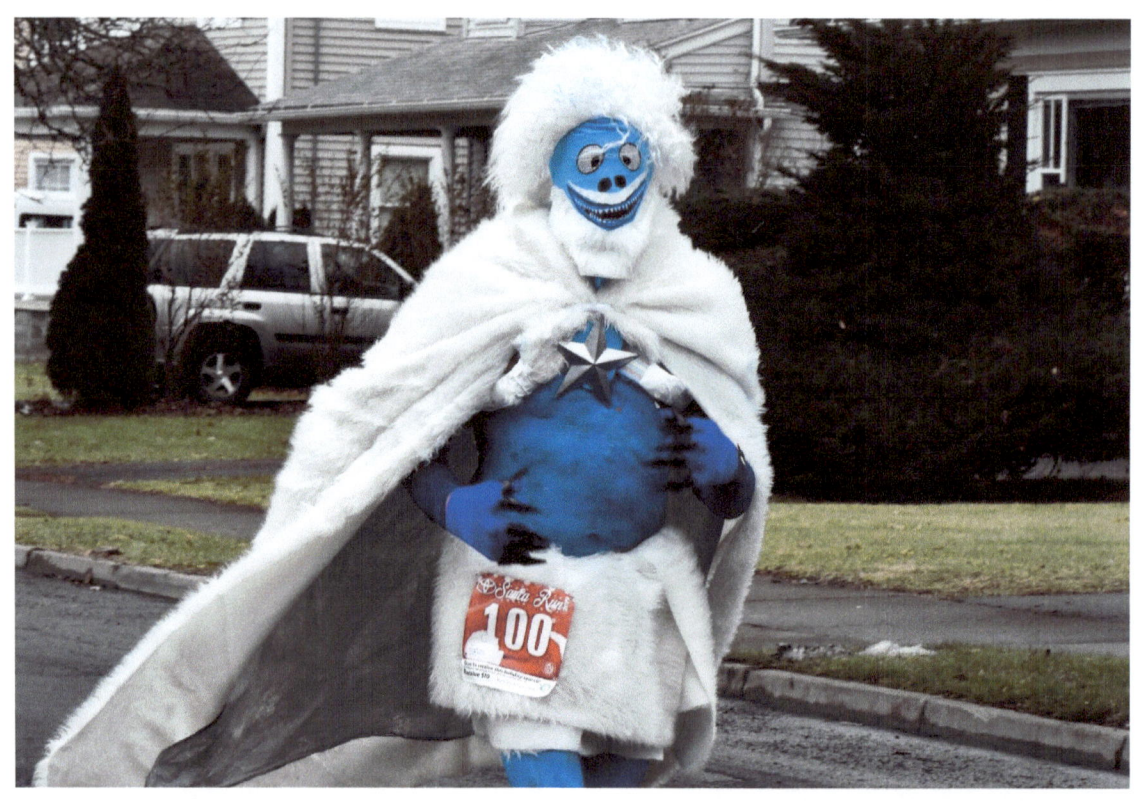
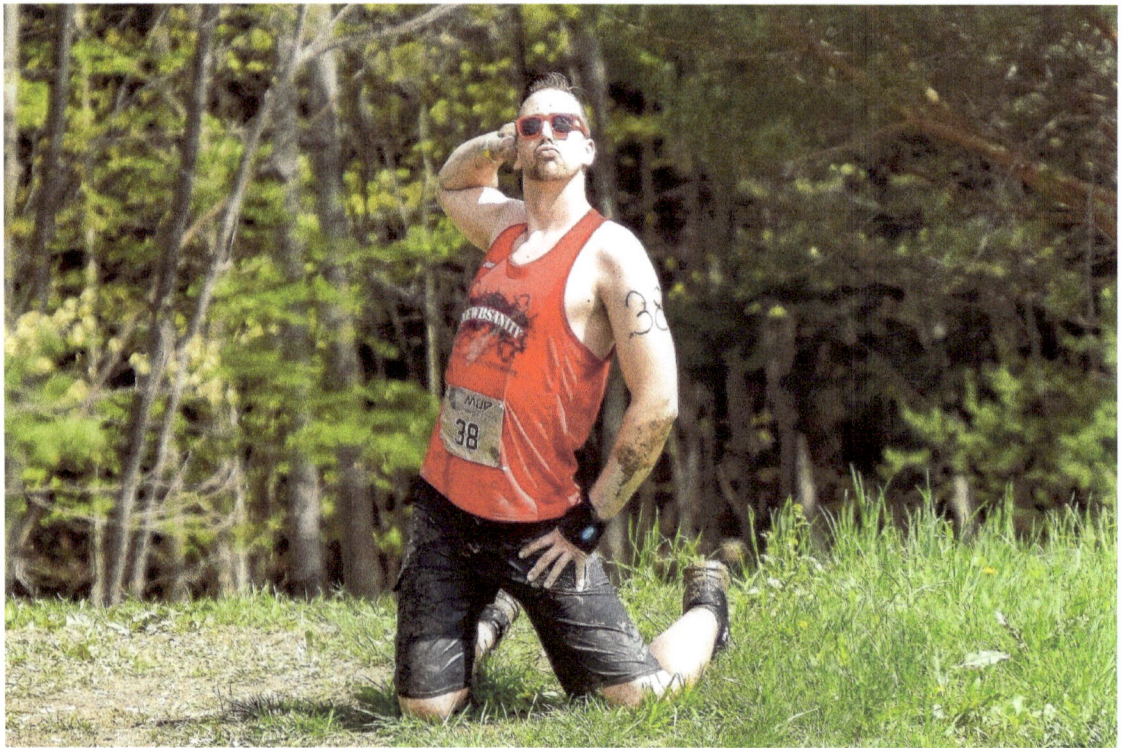

Event Favorites

Over the course of the last six and a half years, I have estimated that I have attended and photographed hundreds of local and regional events. Each and every one of these events yielded a personal favorite. These are just a few that I have come to treasure the most.

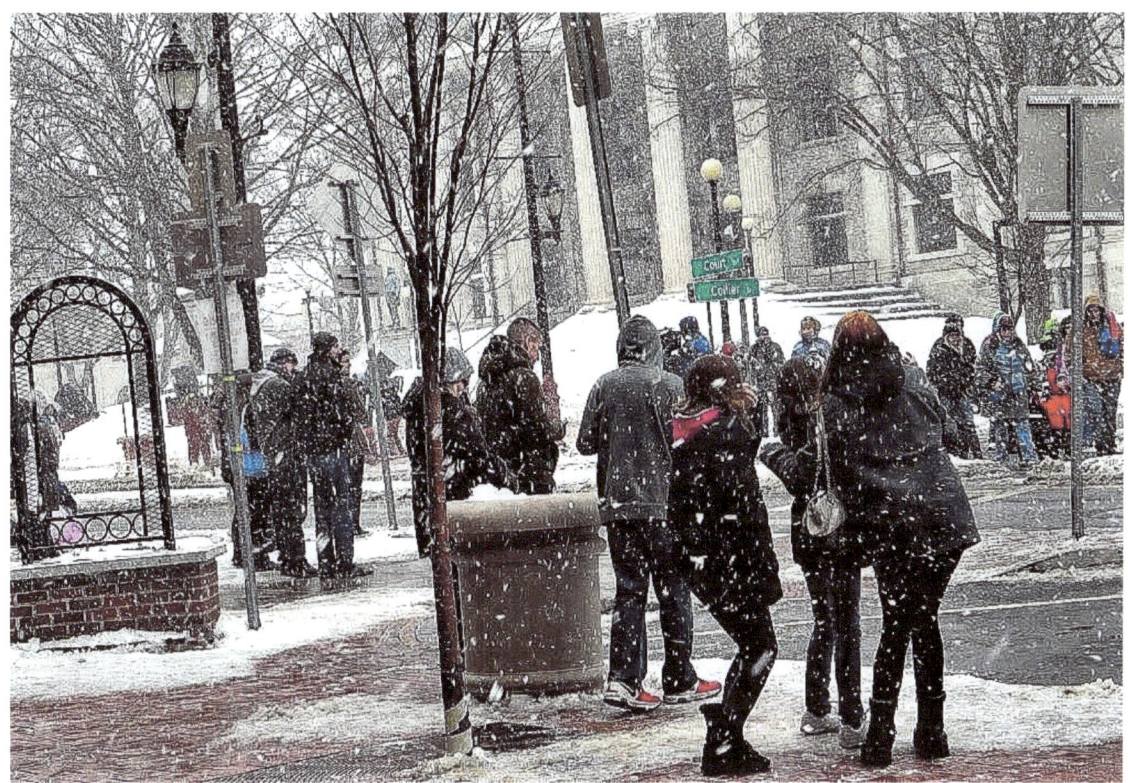

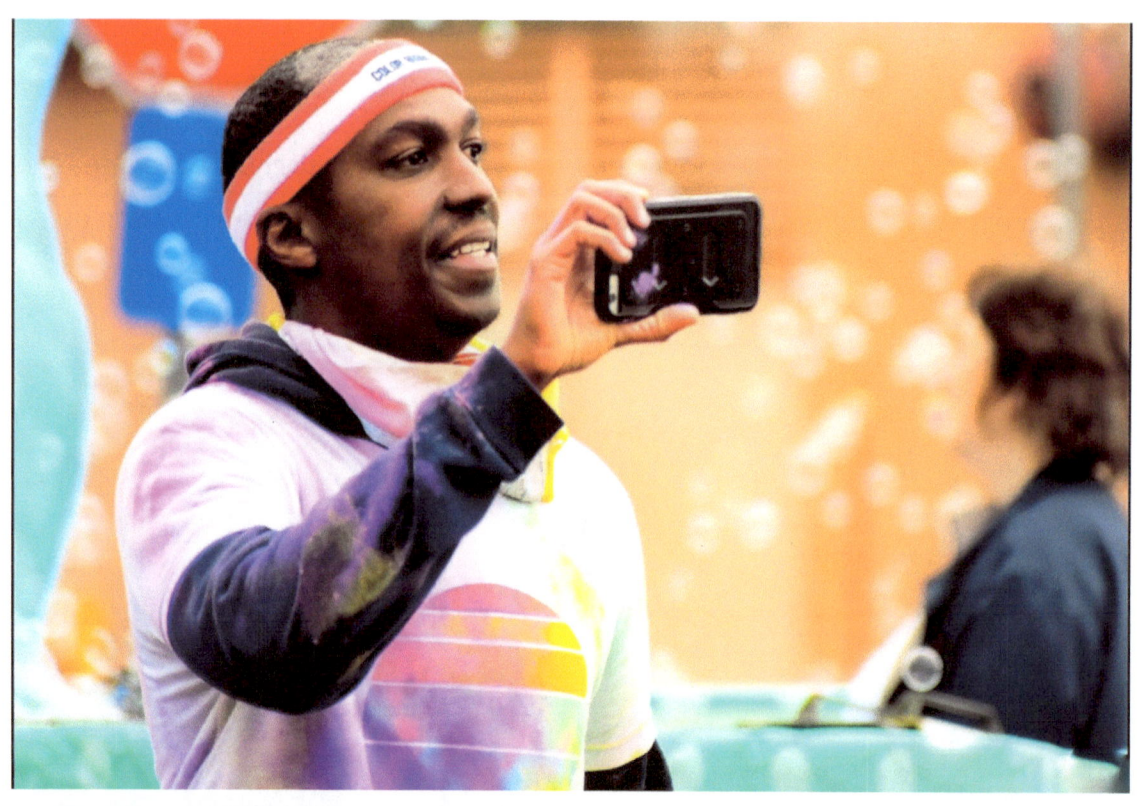
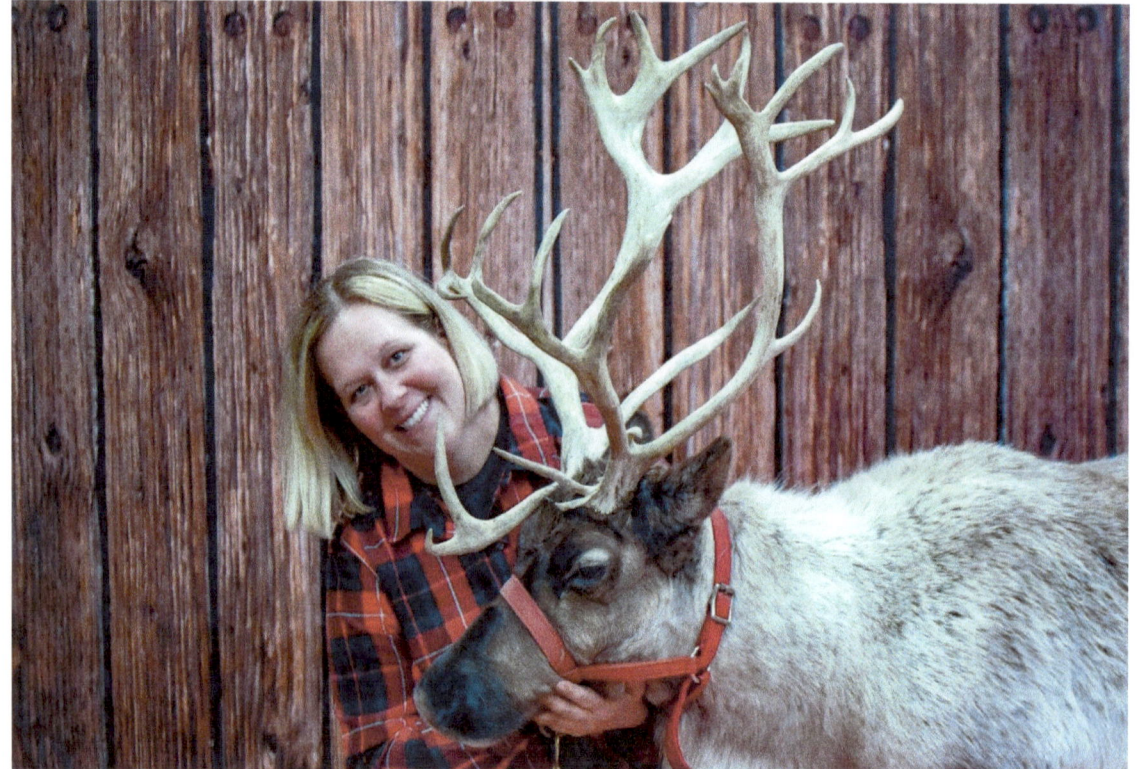

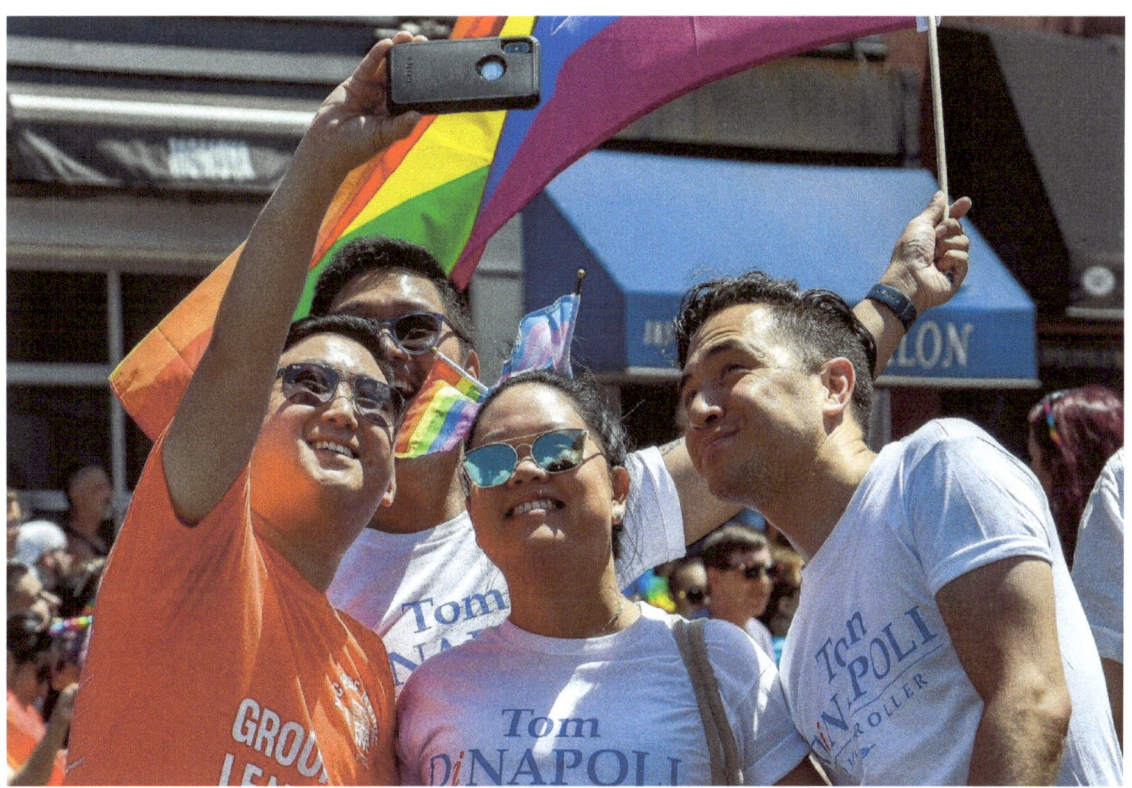
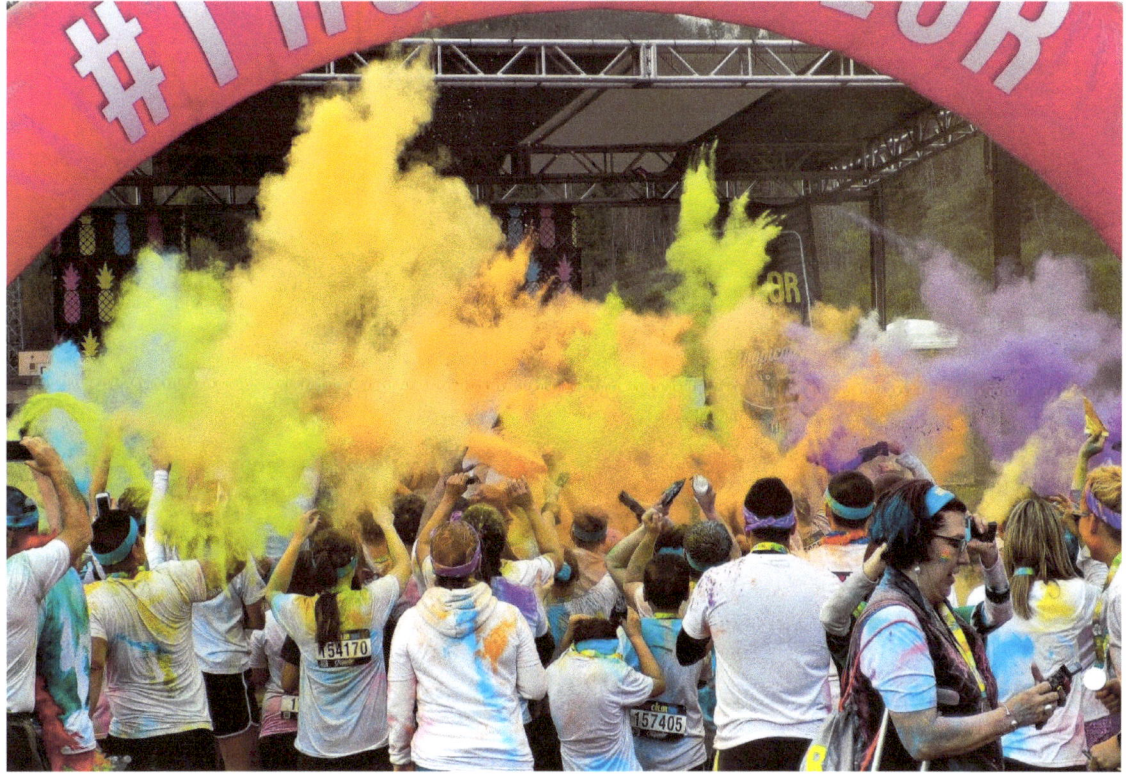

Places

Images of various places and landmarks elicit their own memories in each of us.

Local

Those who follow my adventures on social media are very familiar with my love of the local area here in the Southern Tier of New York. While I have both shared and sold prints of many of the images of local area landmarks, there will always be some that will hold a special place in my heart.

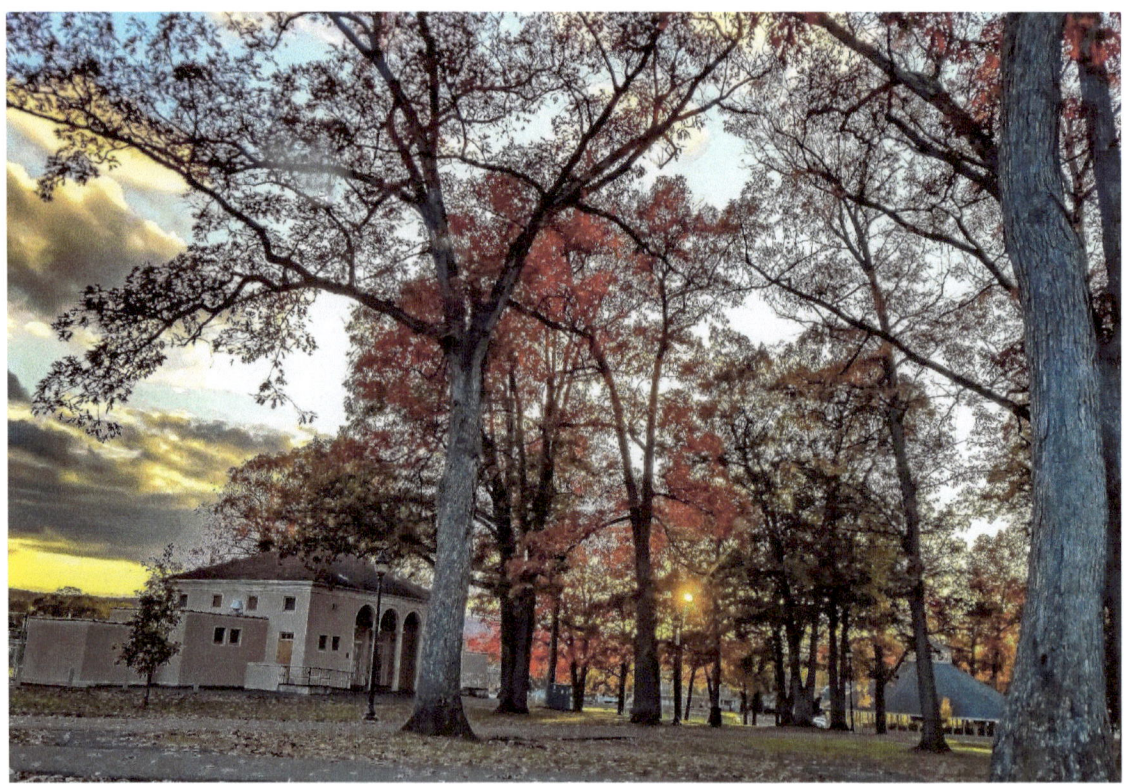

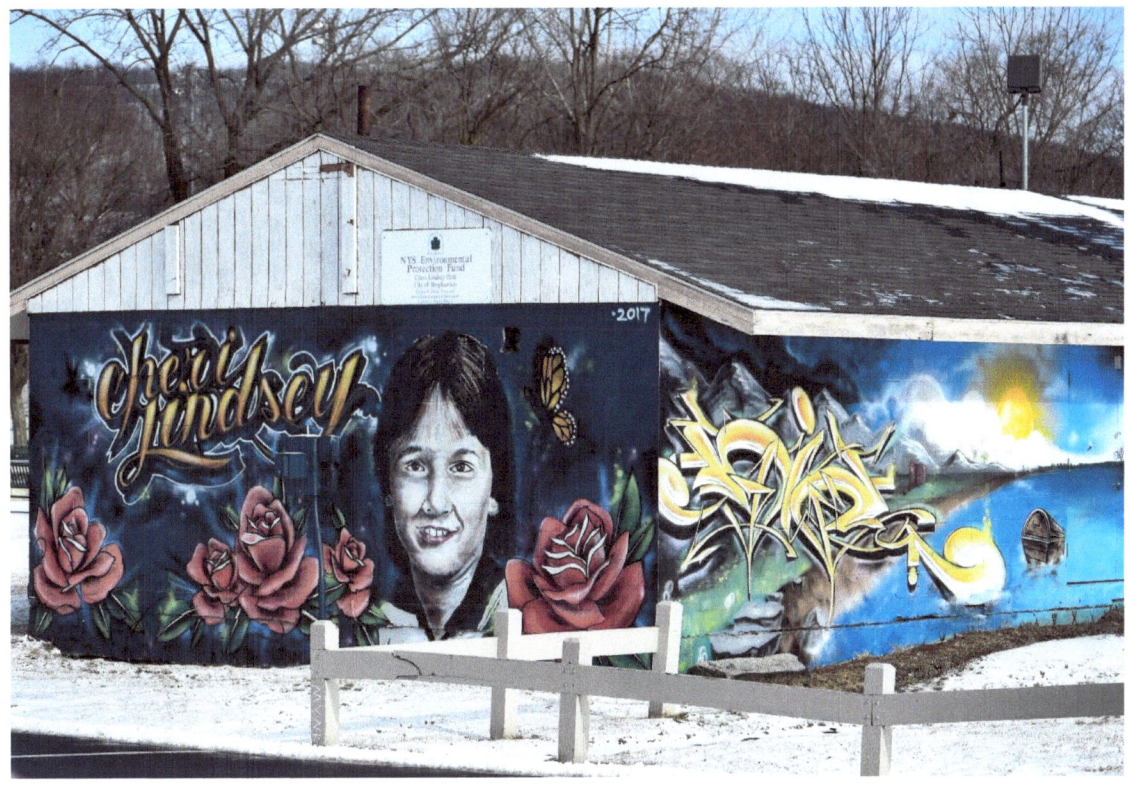

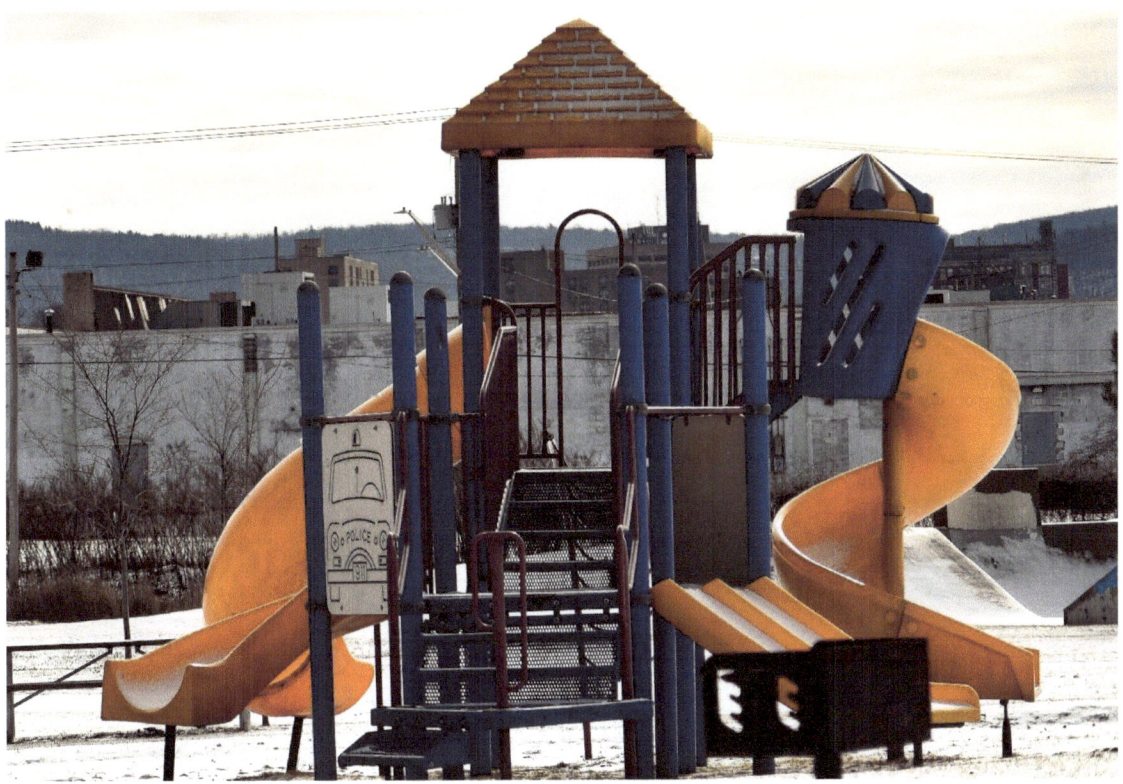

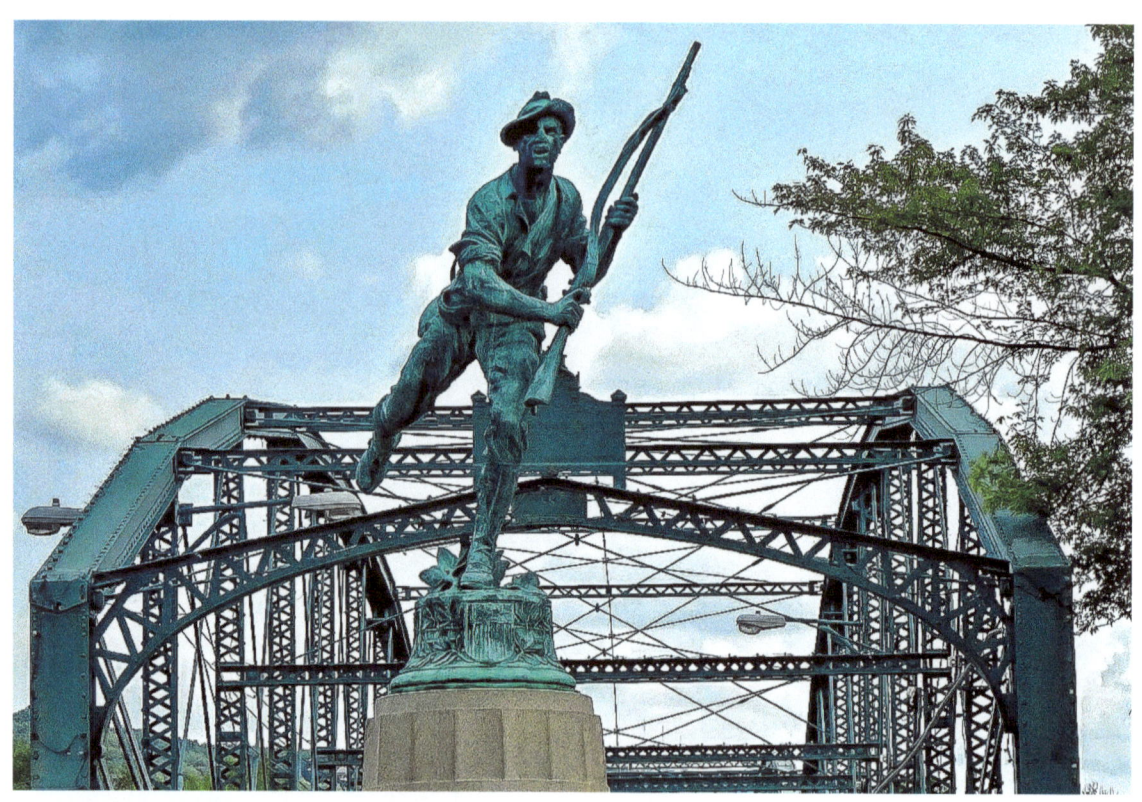

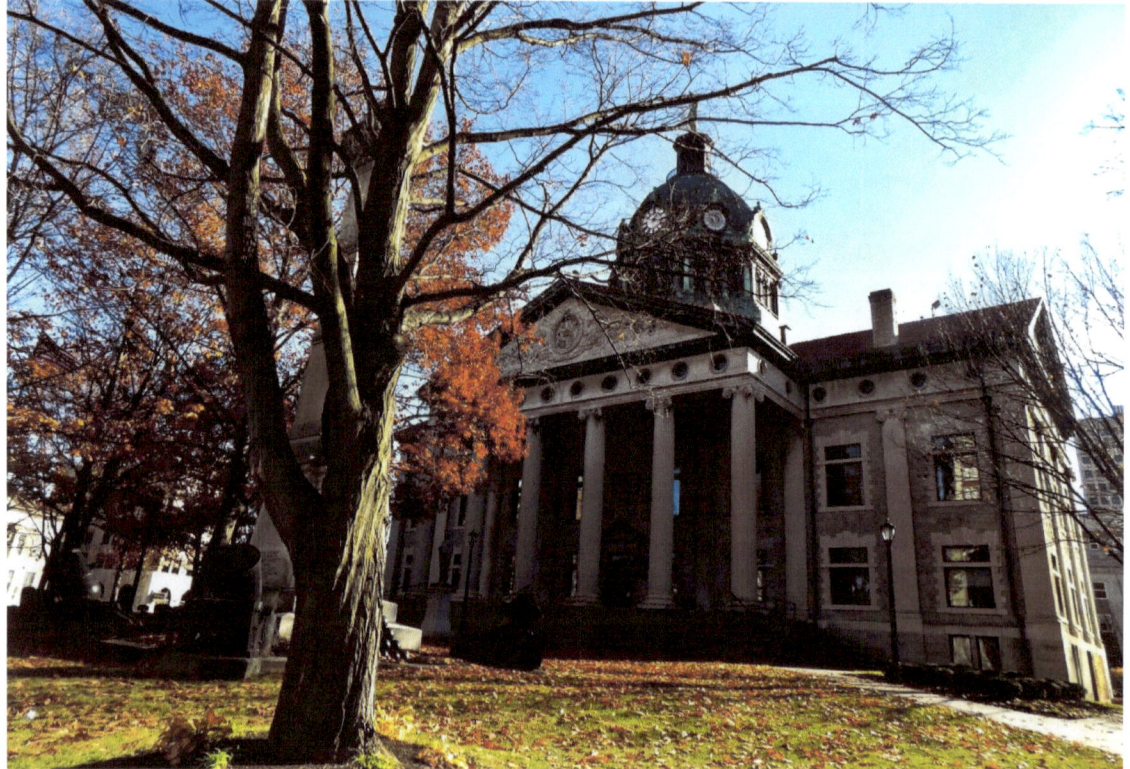

Alexandria Bay (Thousand Islands), NY

Exploring this enchanting area nestled along the St. Lawrence River on the northernmost border of New York State was an experience that I hope to repeat in the future.

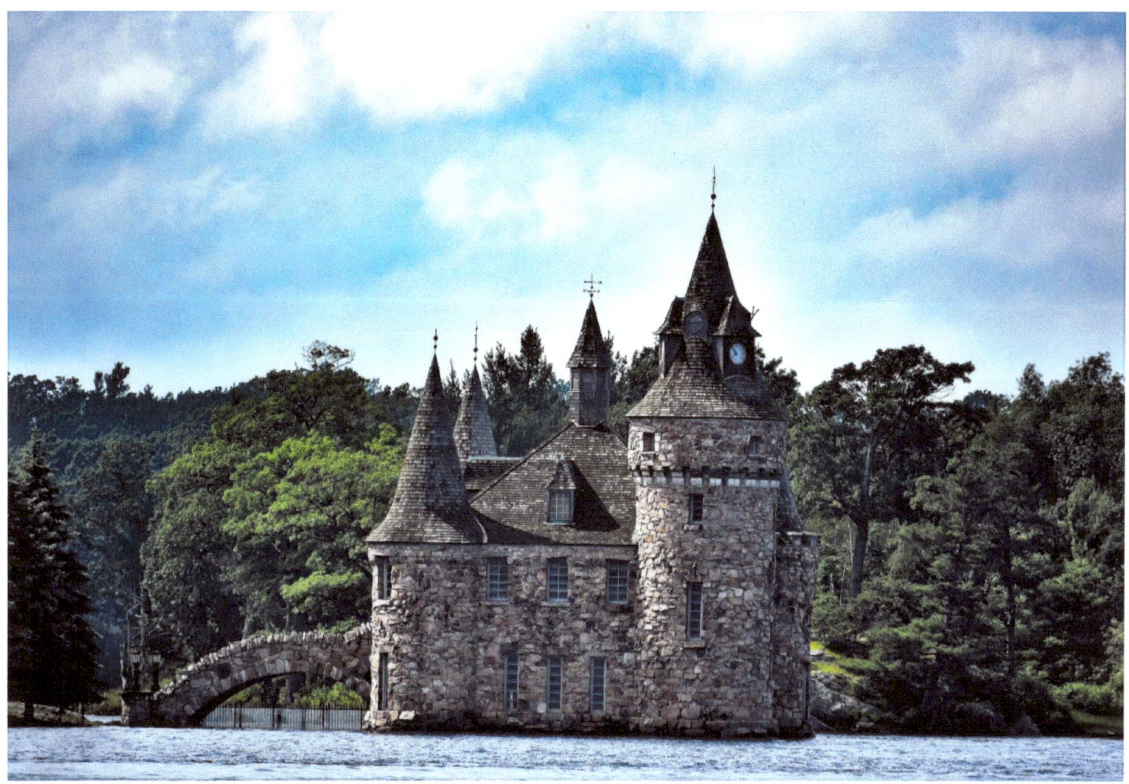

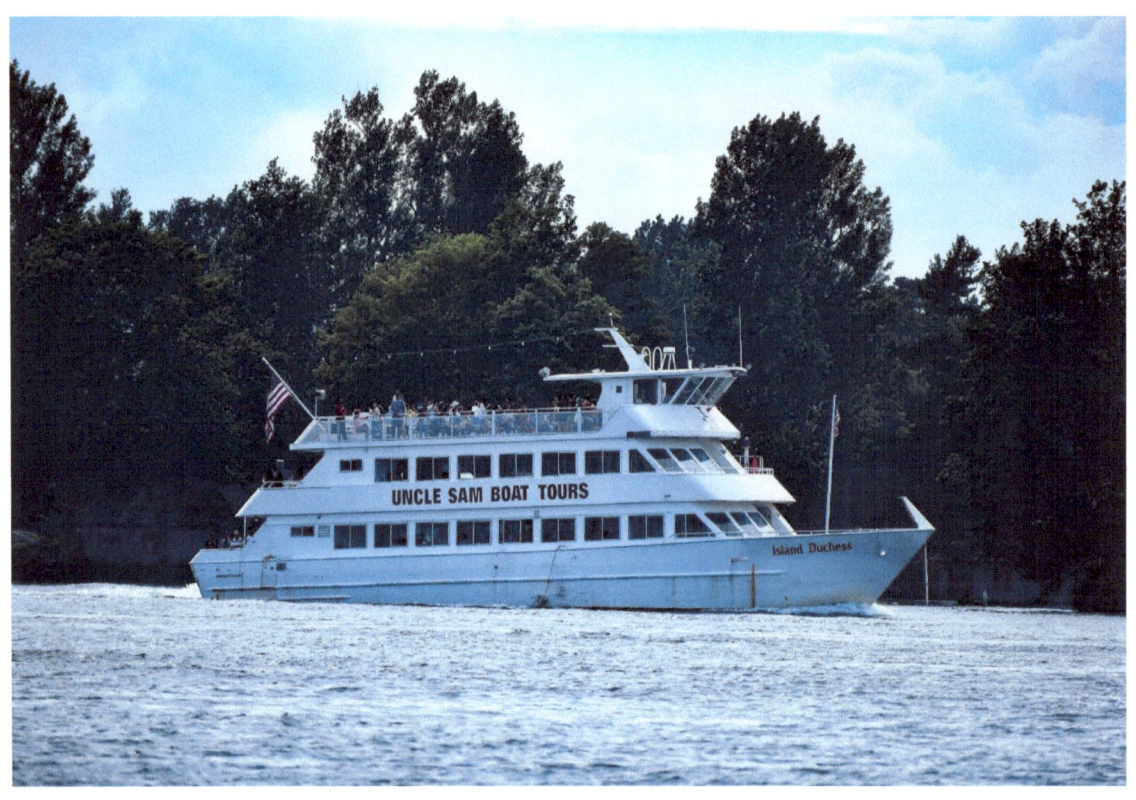

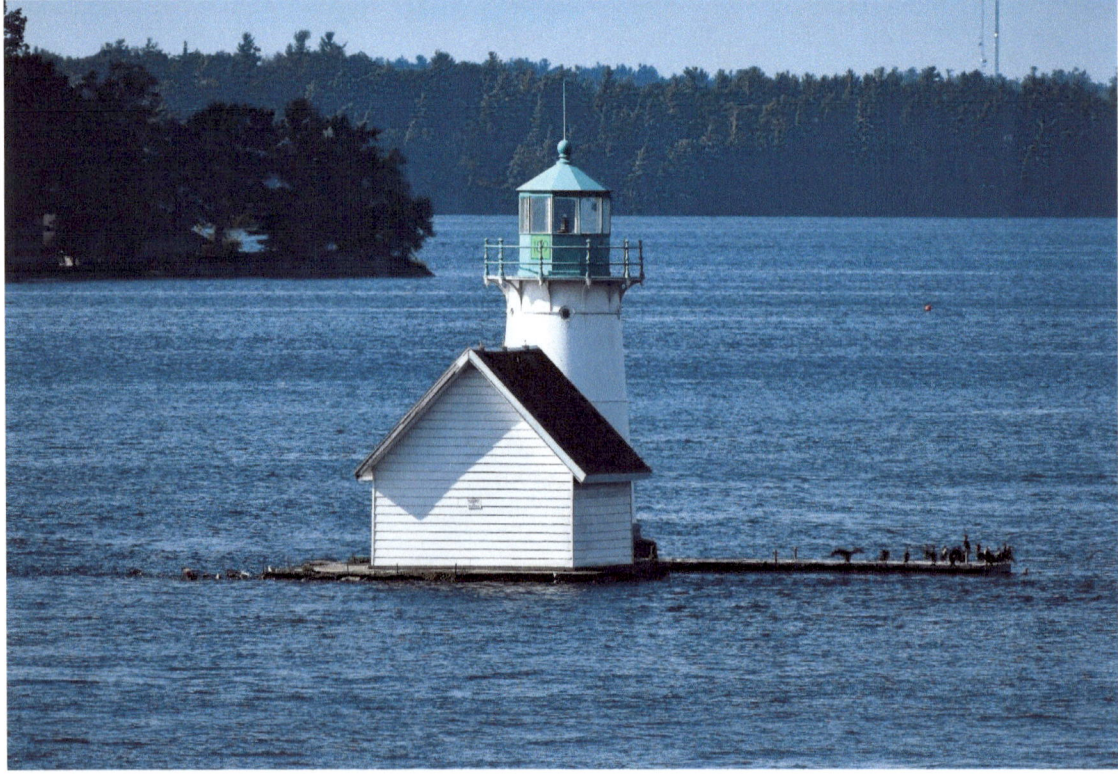

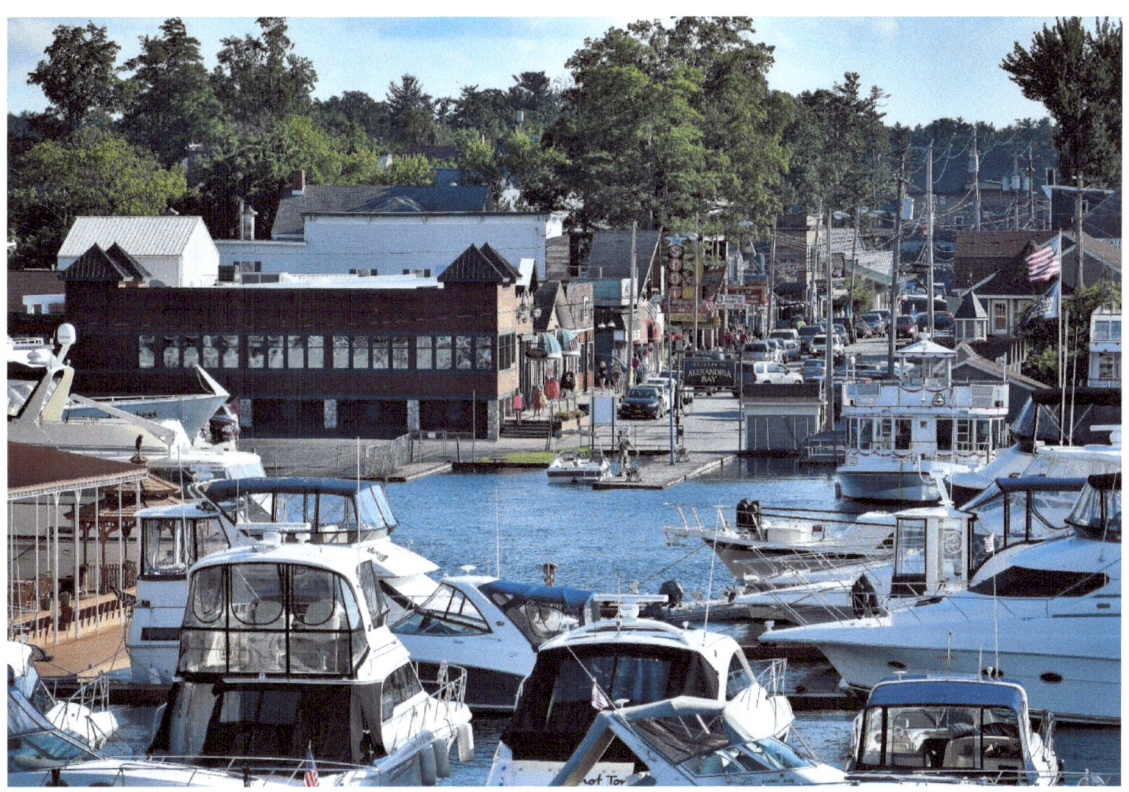
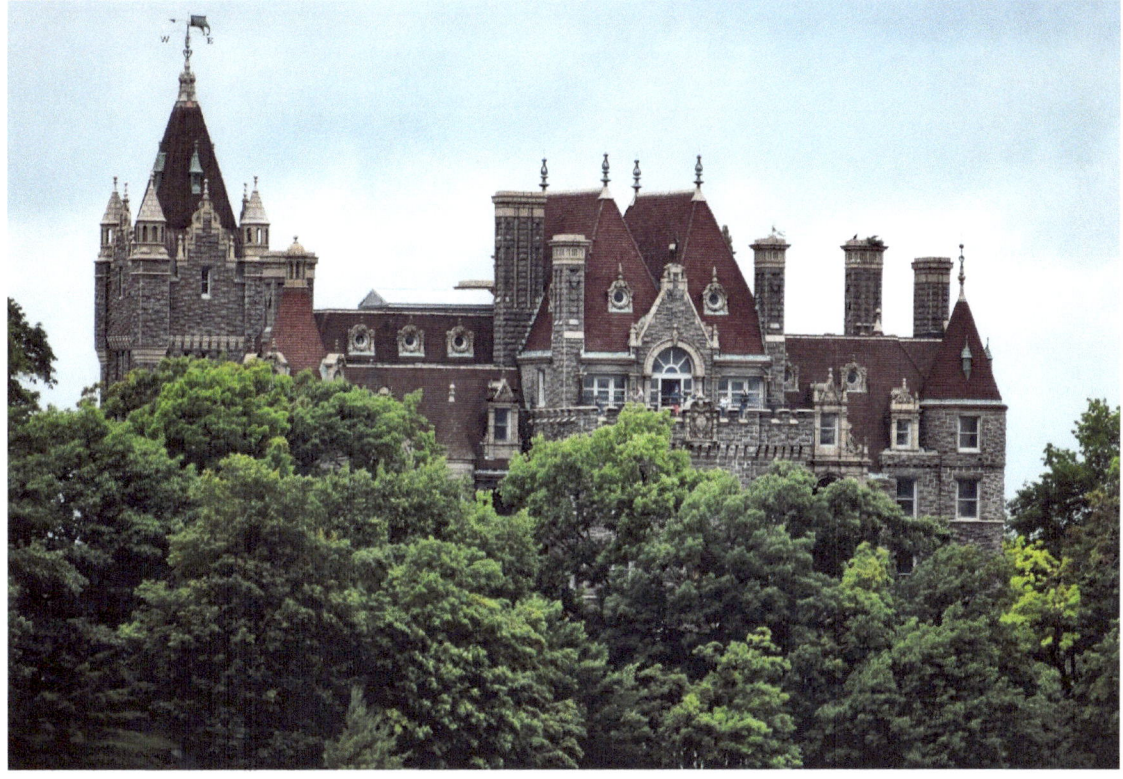

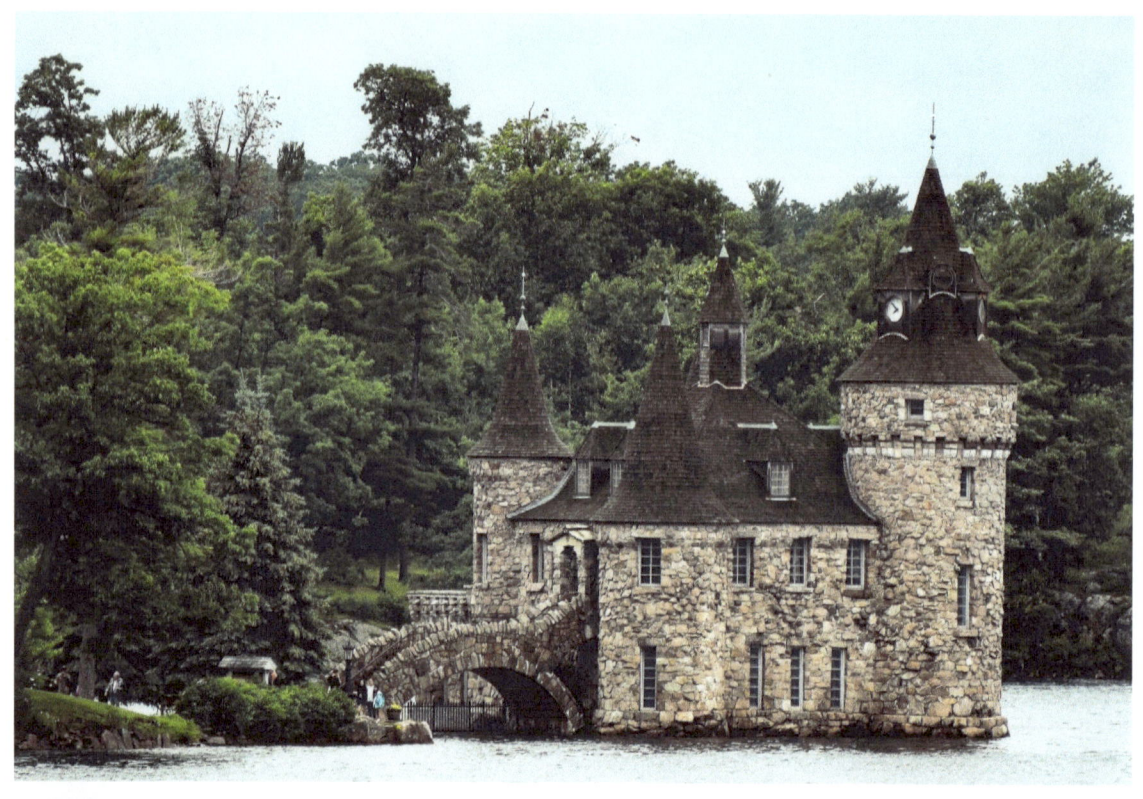

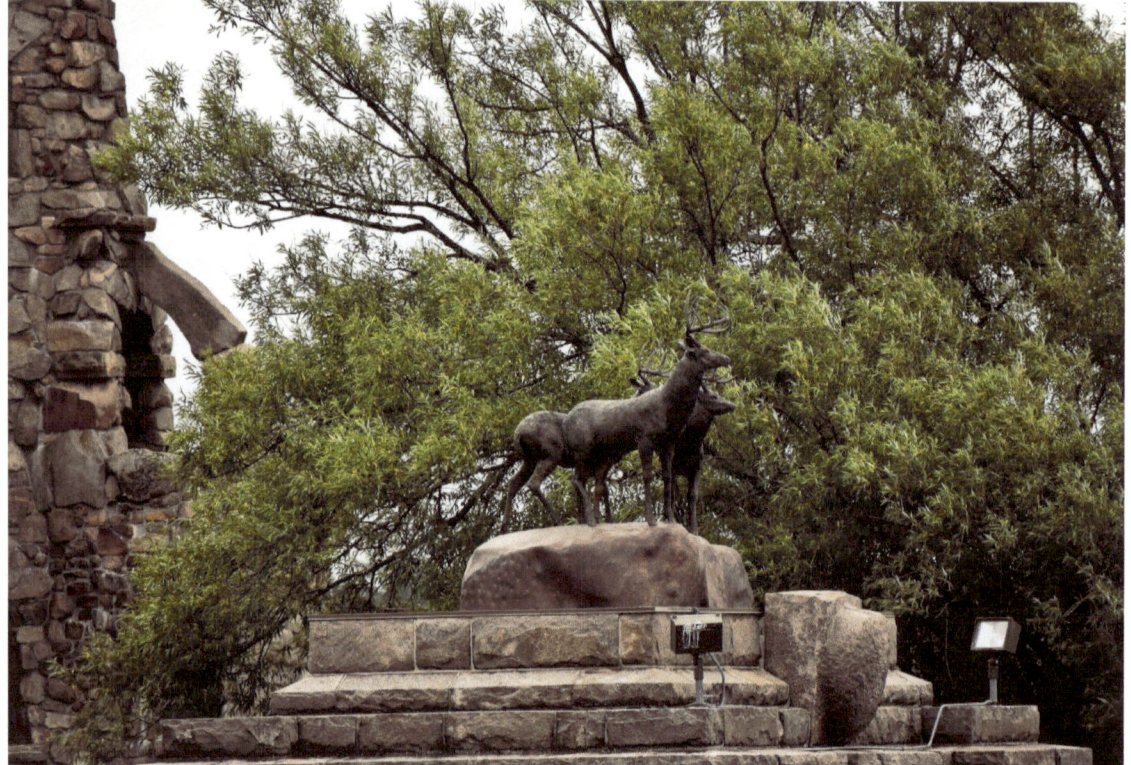

New York City

Nothing is more iconic than images of New York City. While none of these are unique, they rank up there as some of my favorites.

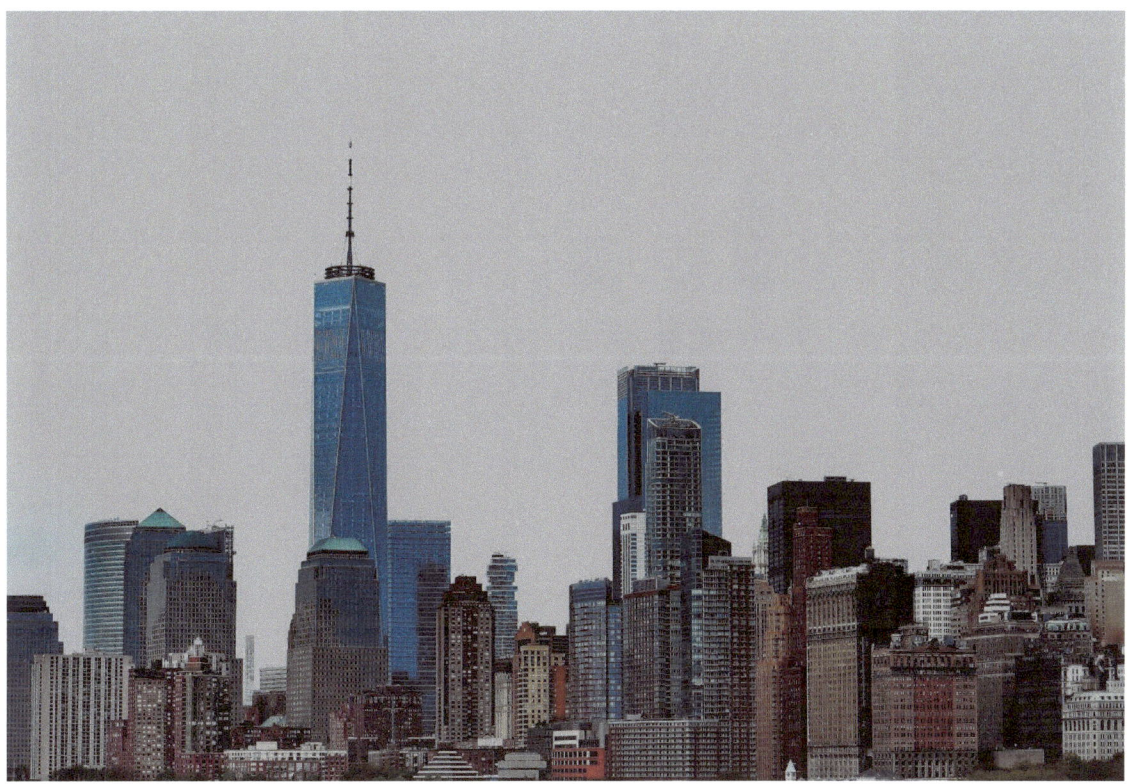

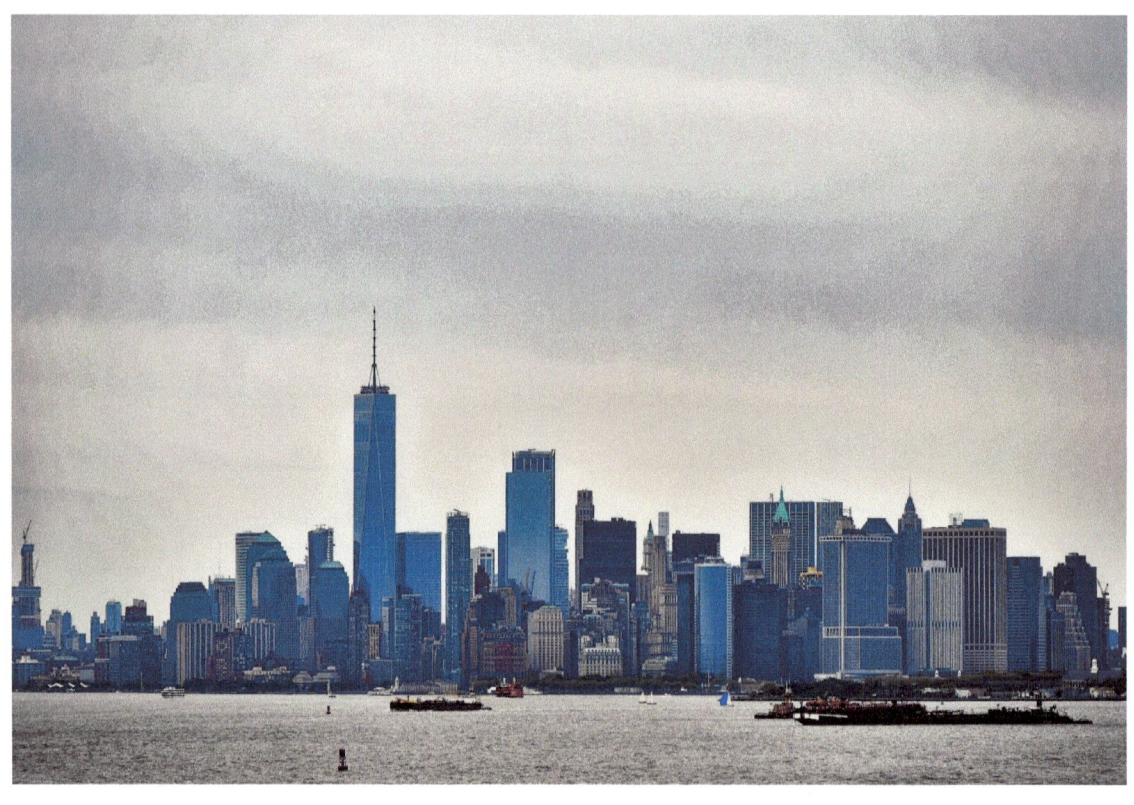

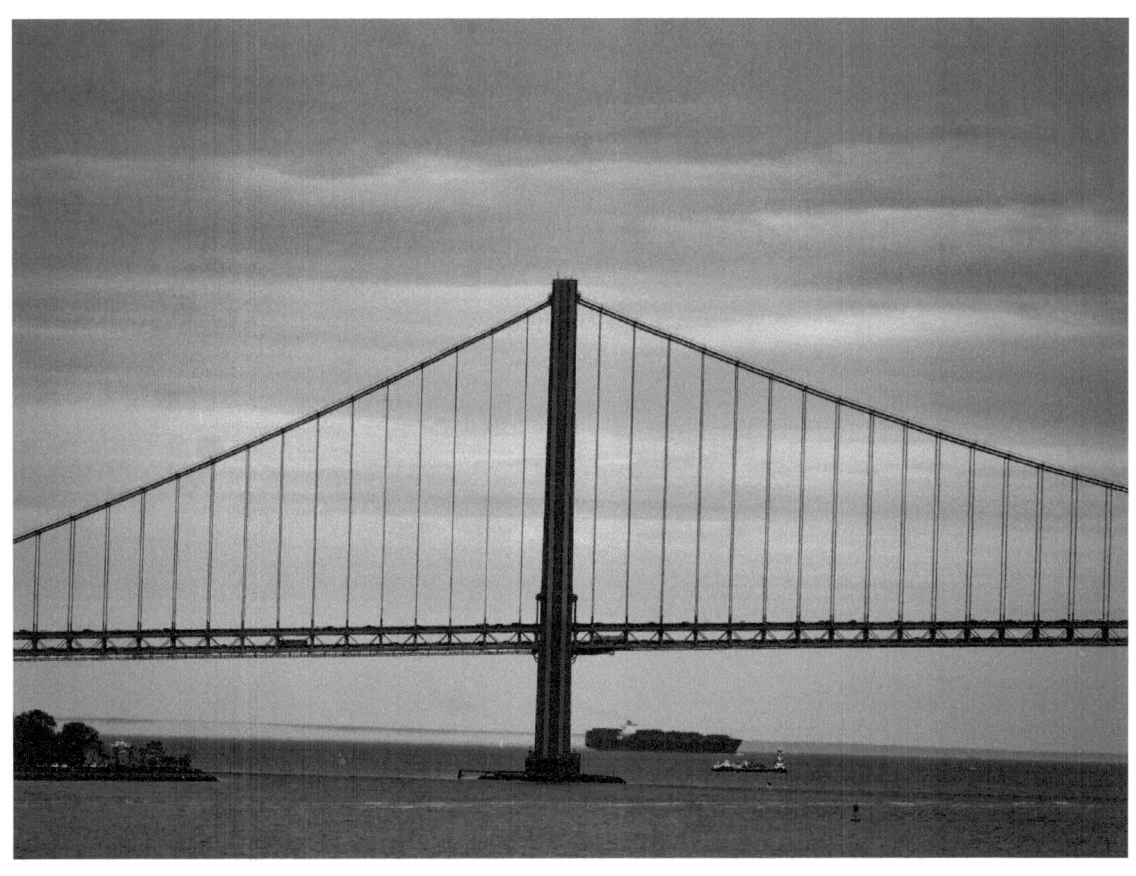

Cape Canaveral, Florida

The east coast of Florida is home to expansive beaches and, of course, Kennedy Space Center. Returning to the Space Center after over 30 years, brought back some very personal feelings of nostalgia.

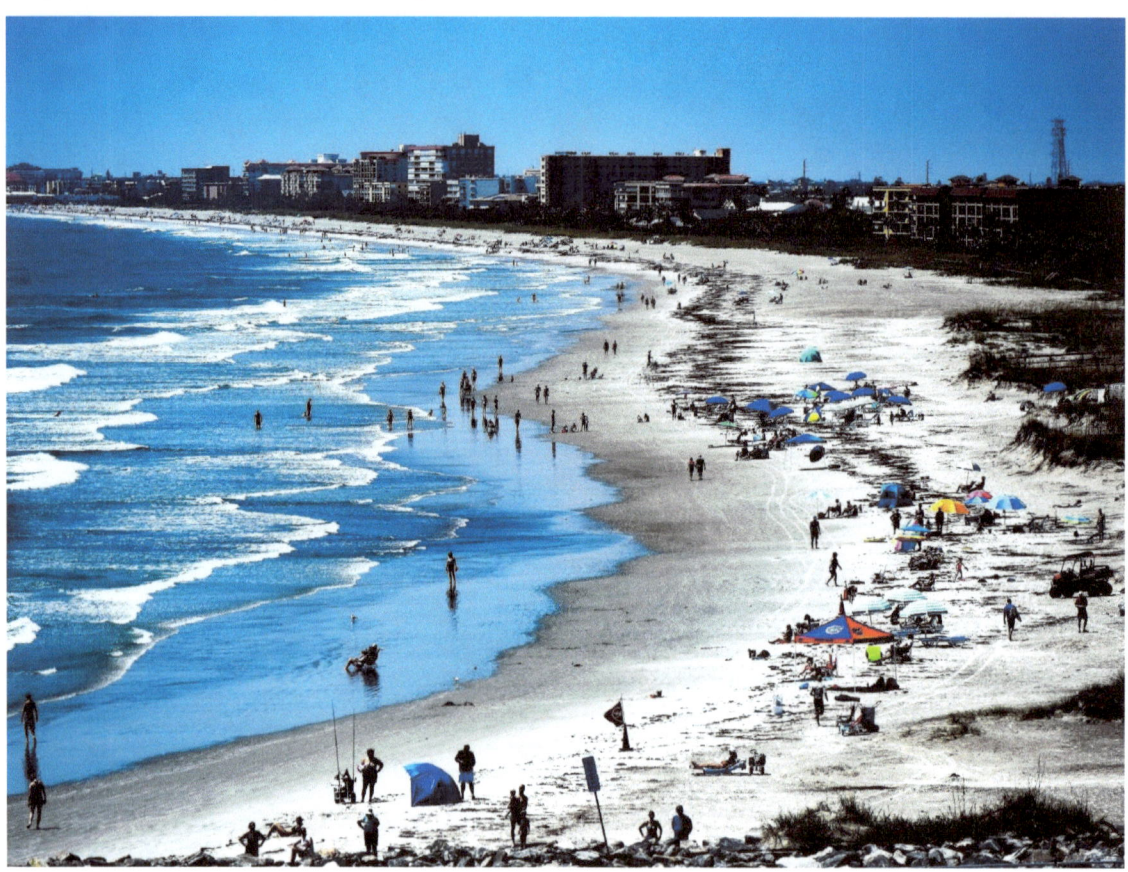

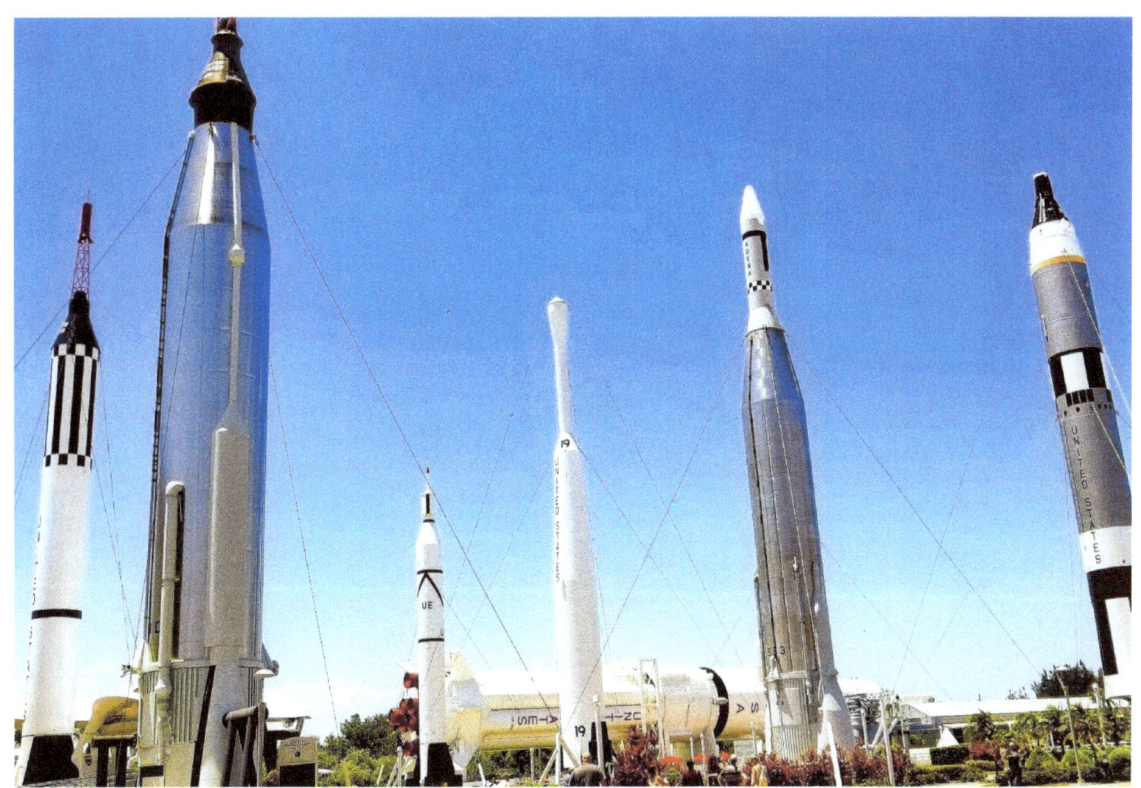

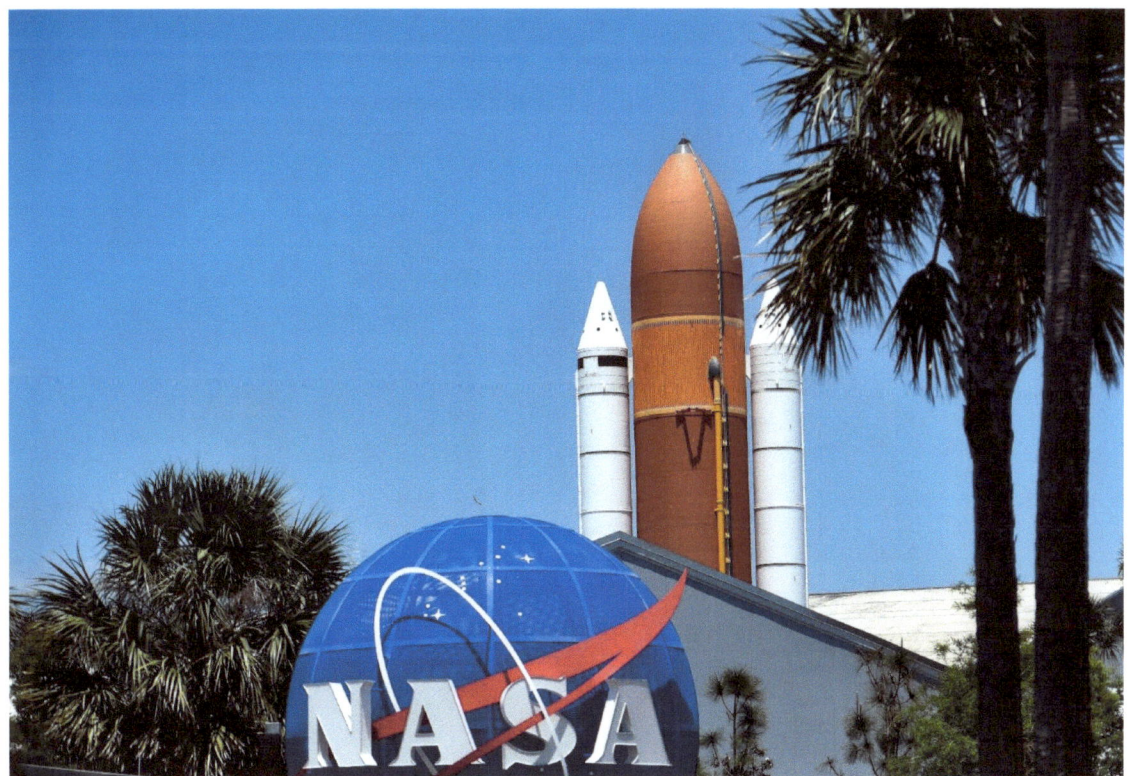

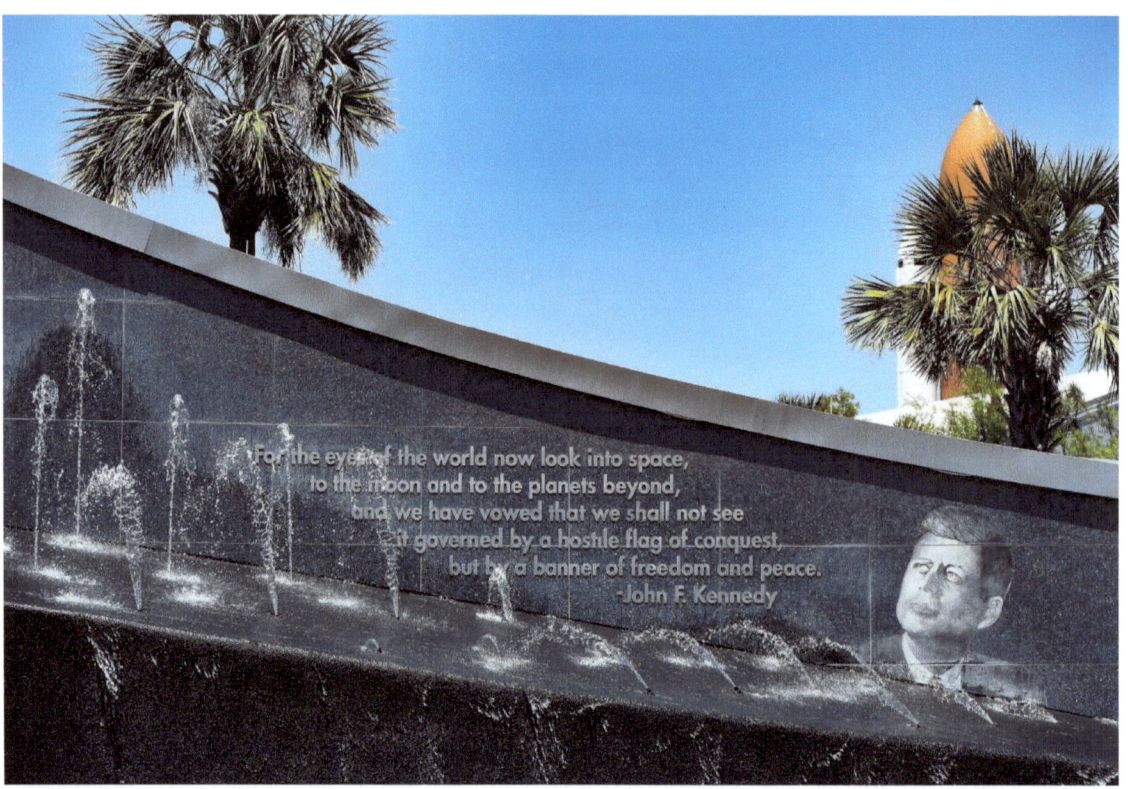

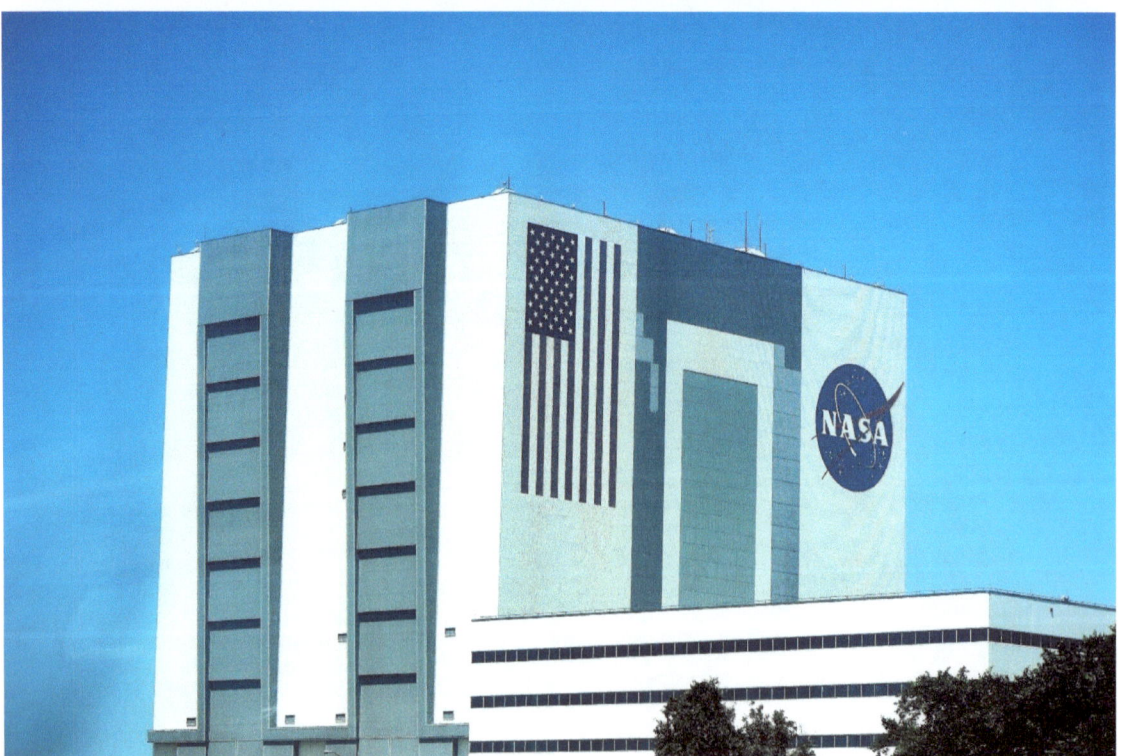

Nassau, The Bahamas

I'm going to let you in on a little secret, I am mildly obsessed with Nassau. Everytime I have visited, I find myself in my "happy" place. I long for the day when I can spend some more time there.

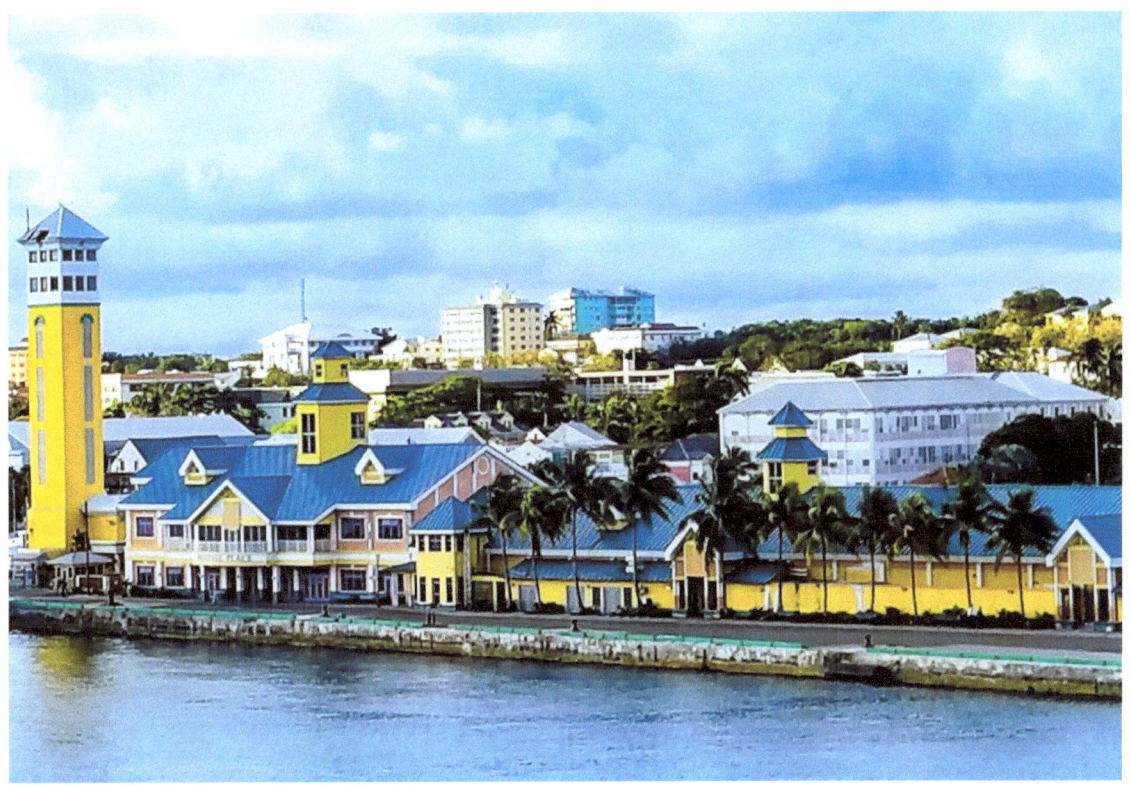

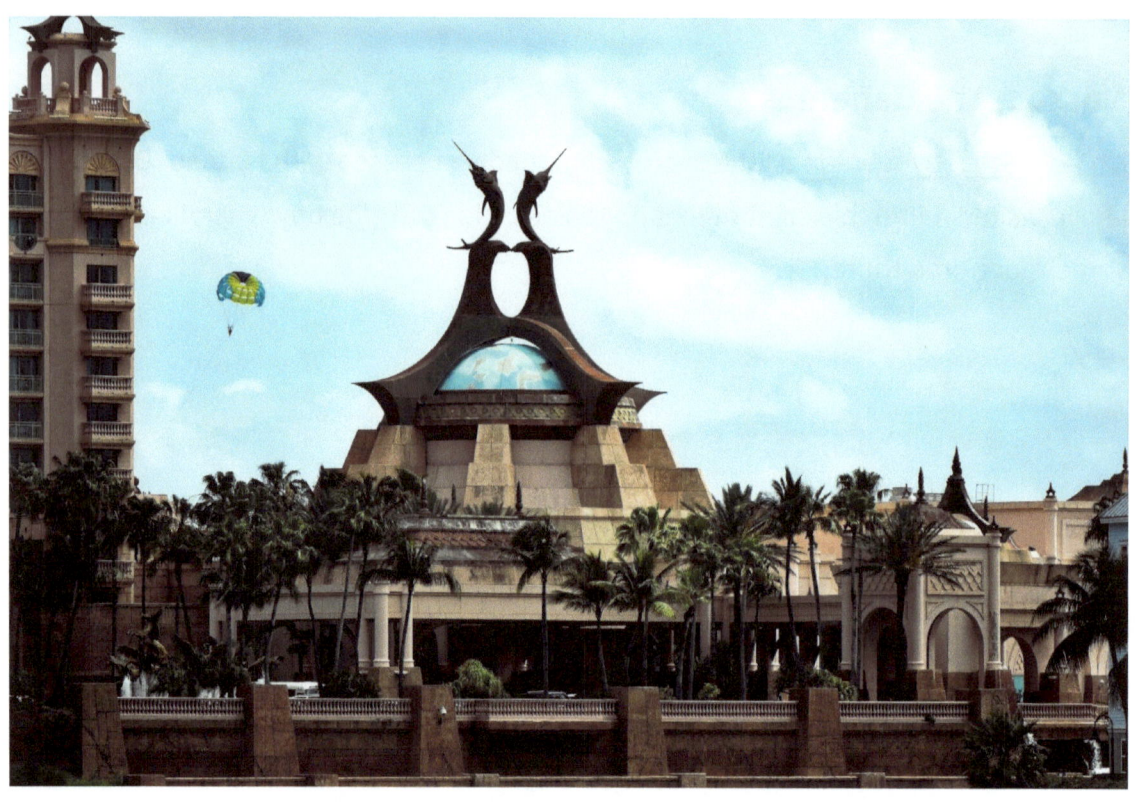

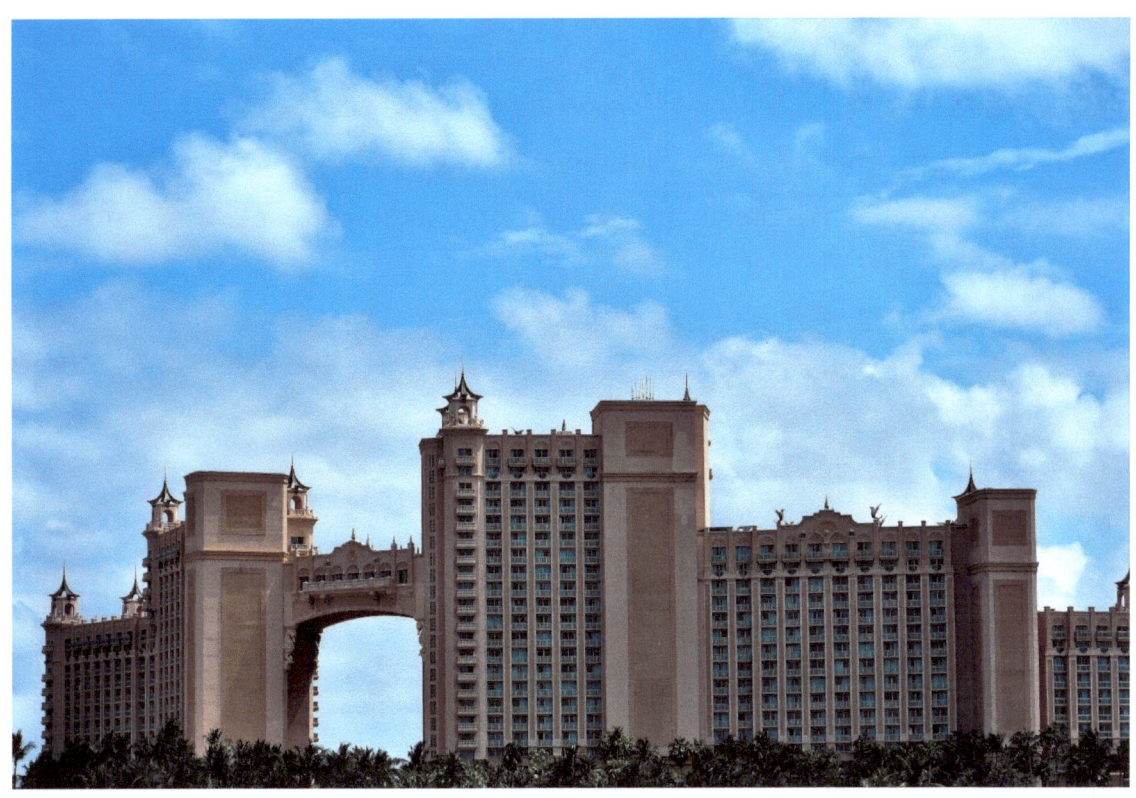
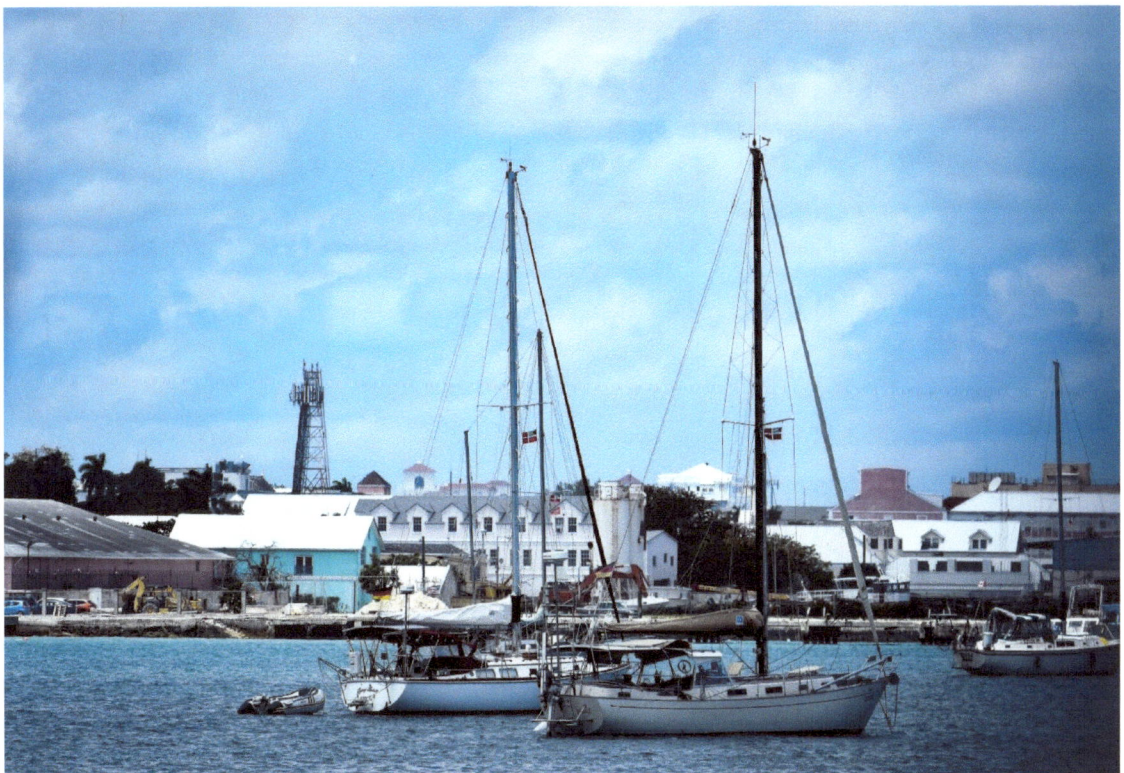

The Finger Lakes

The Finger Lakes region of New York is renowned for its wineries and its lakes. It contains some of the most beautiful waterfalls and water features in the Northeast surrounded by rich farmland.

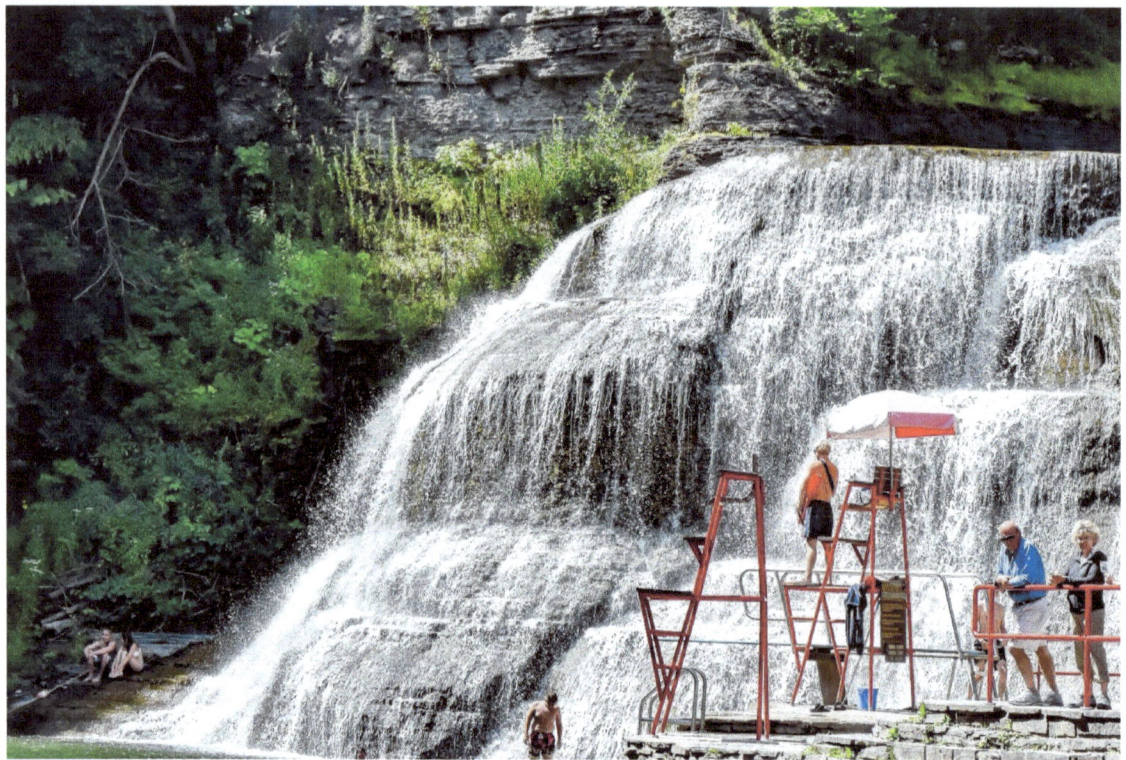

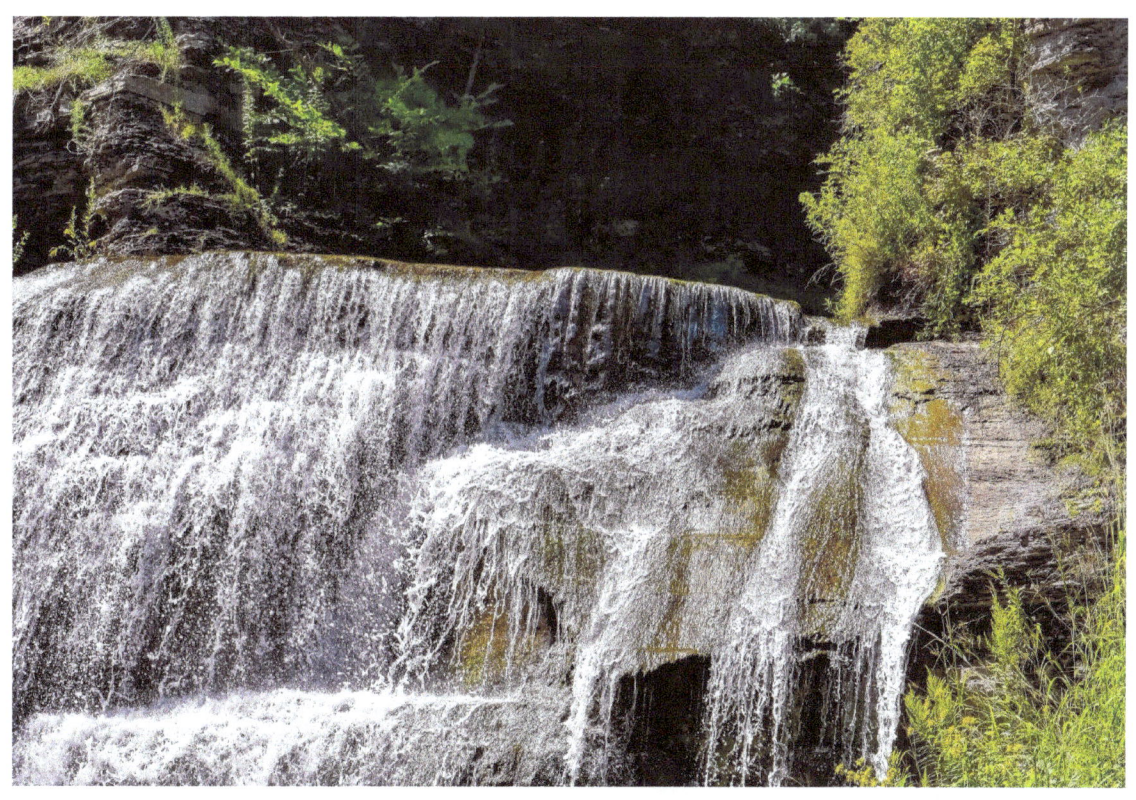
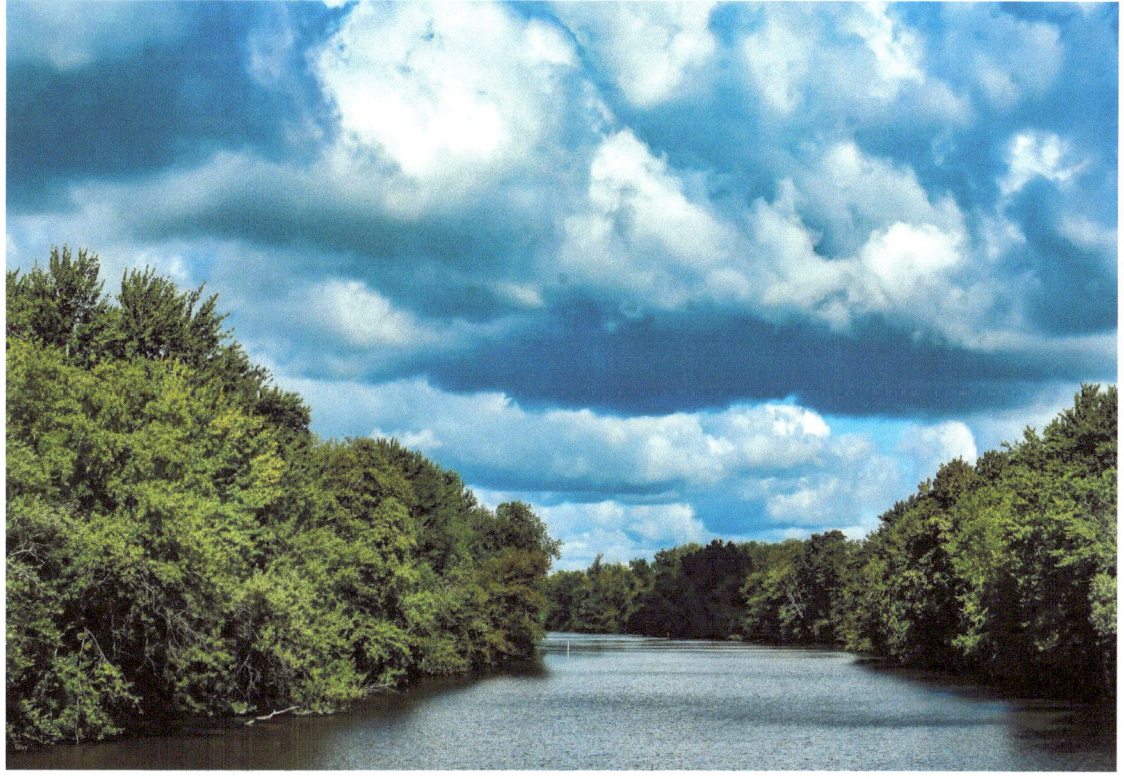

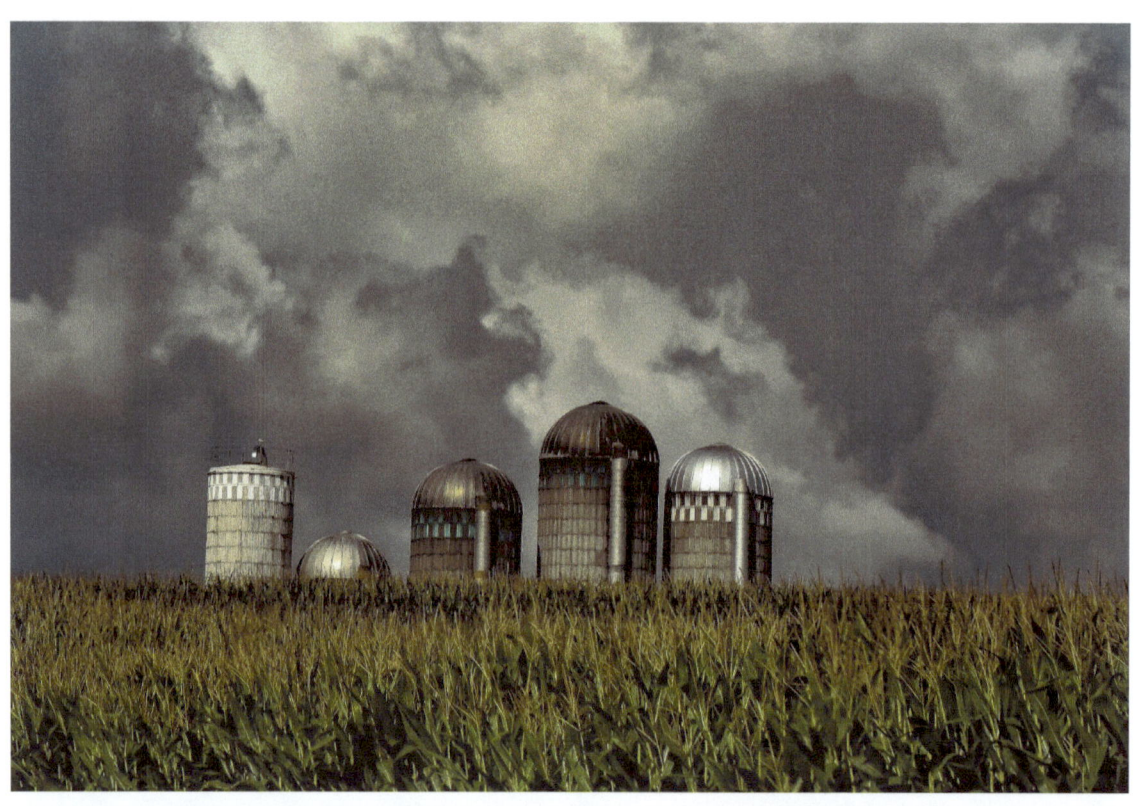
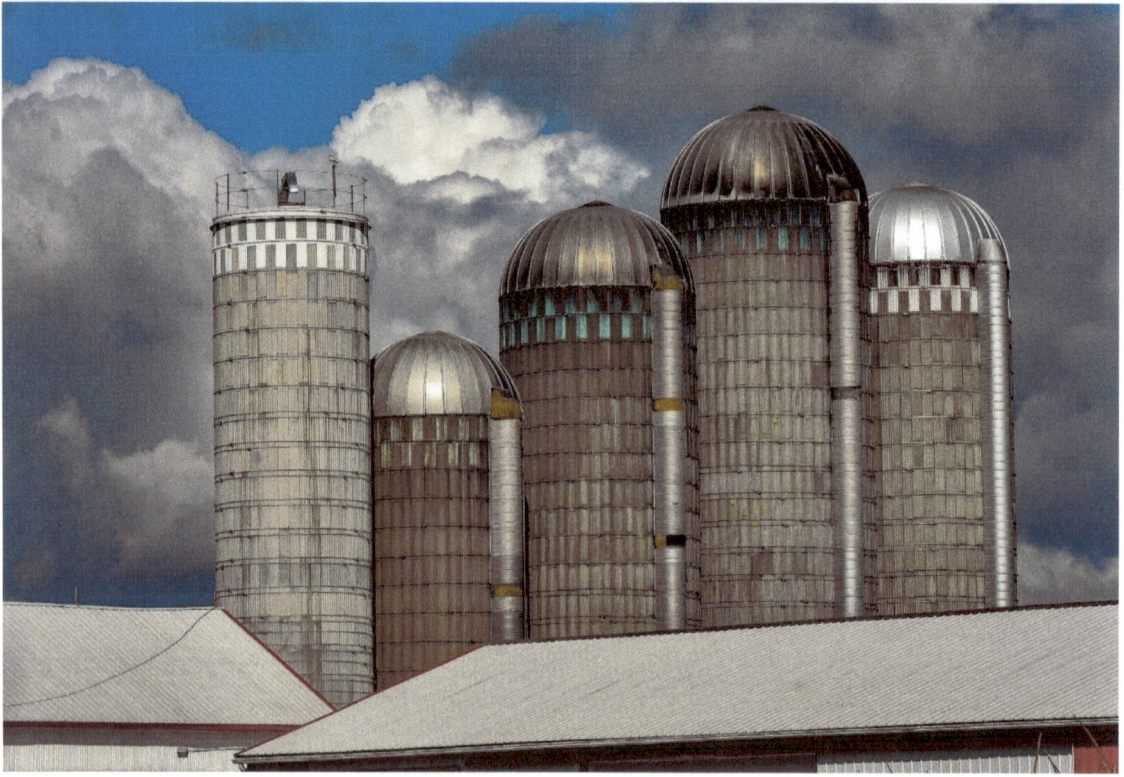

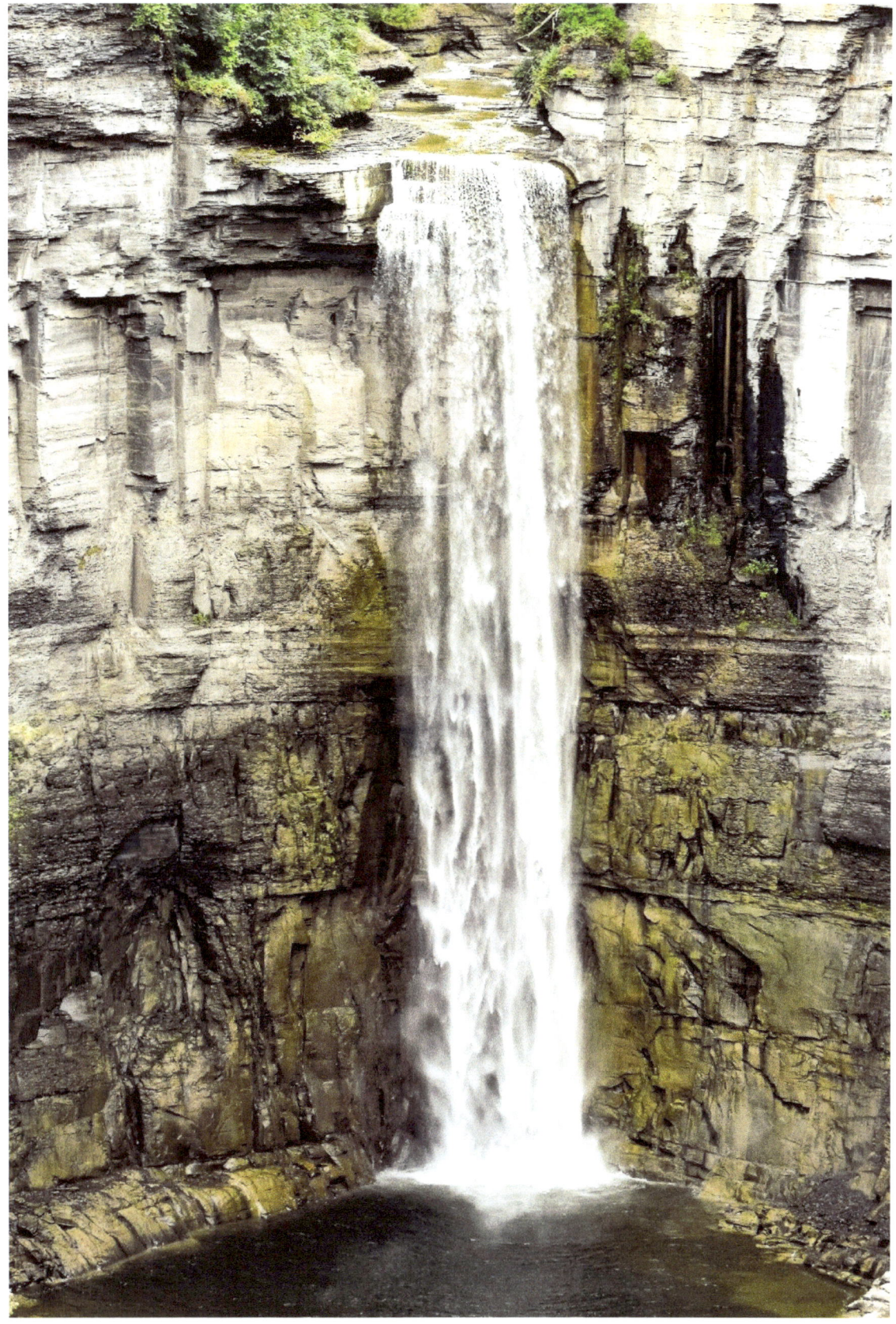

Things

More often than not, my lens has been drawn to, for lack of a better word, things. I find myself focused on the unusual, unexpected, furry, feathery and floral.

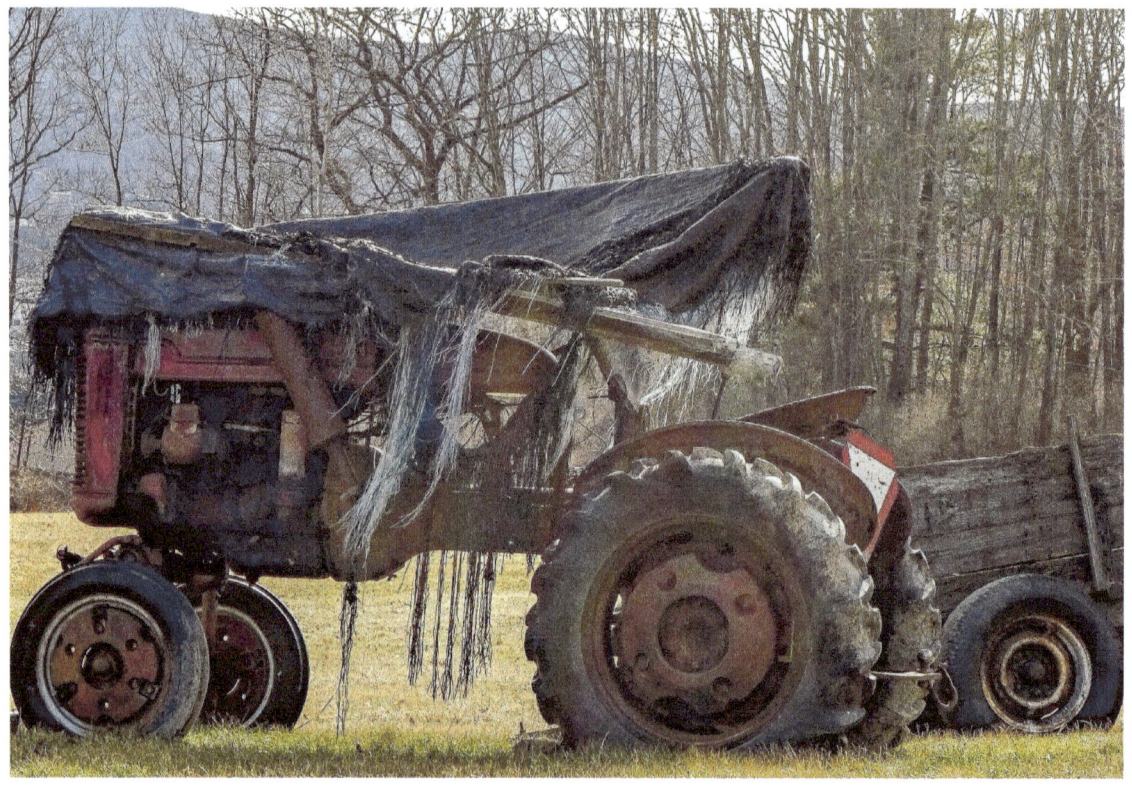

Unusual and Unexpected

One example is the time I came across these two cards arranged in an empty planter. What was their purpose? Was it a sign or just a happy coincidence?

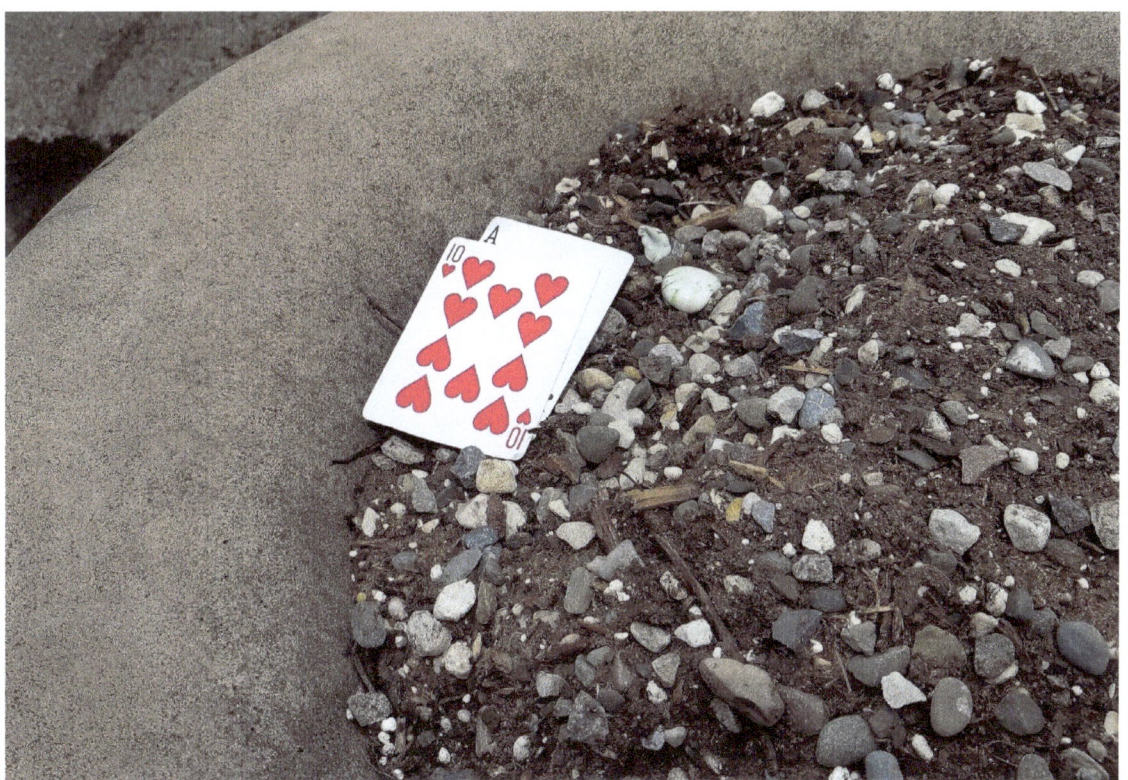

Then there was this shot I captured during a break from a photoshoot for a local band's CD artwork. There was just something about how these props were arranged on the table that drew my lens to focus on the image.

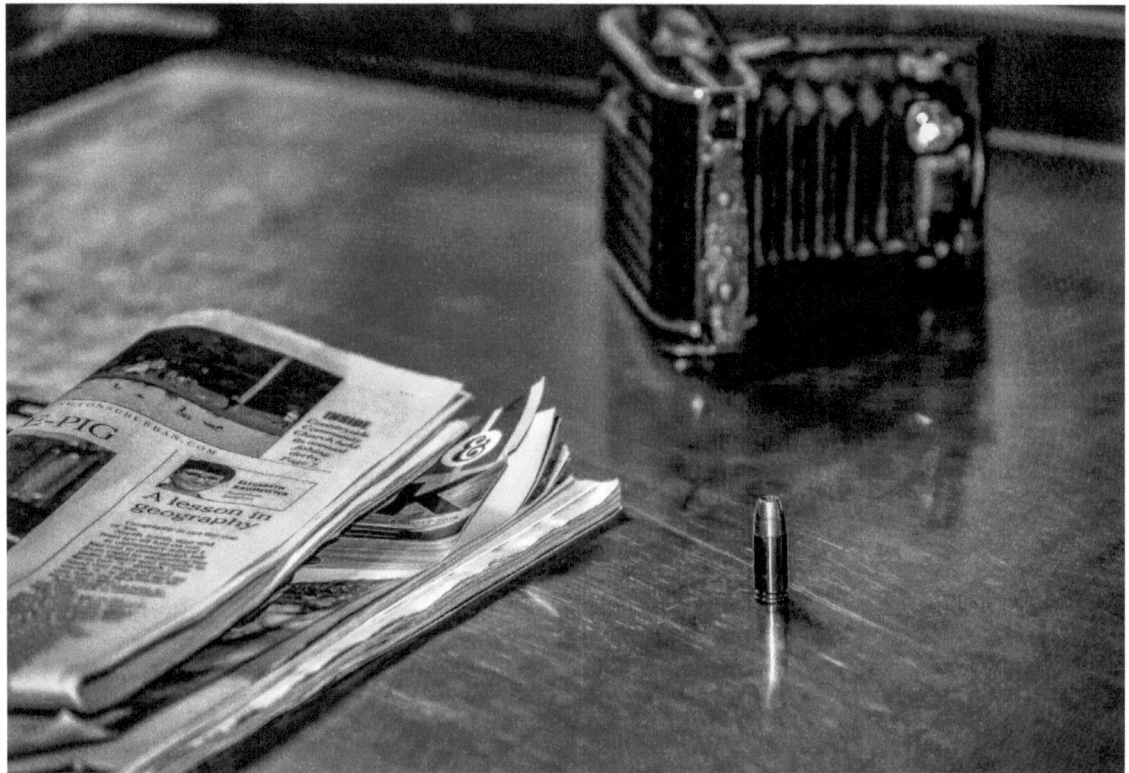

Not everyone obeys traffic signs as evidenced by this shot taken during one of my many walks downtown.

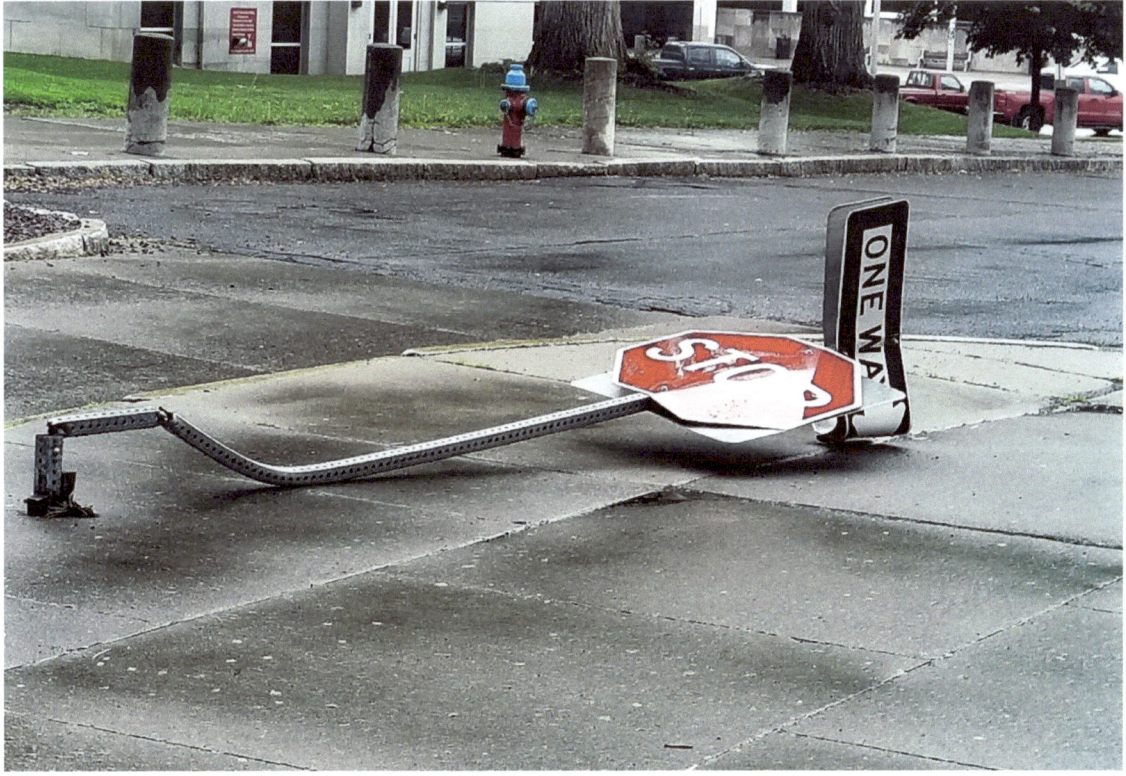

Here are just a few more of my unusual and unexpected favorites.

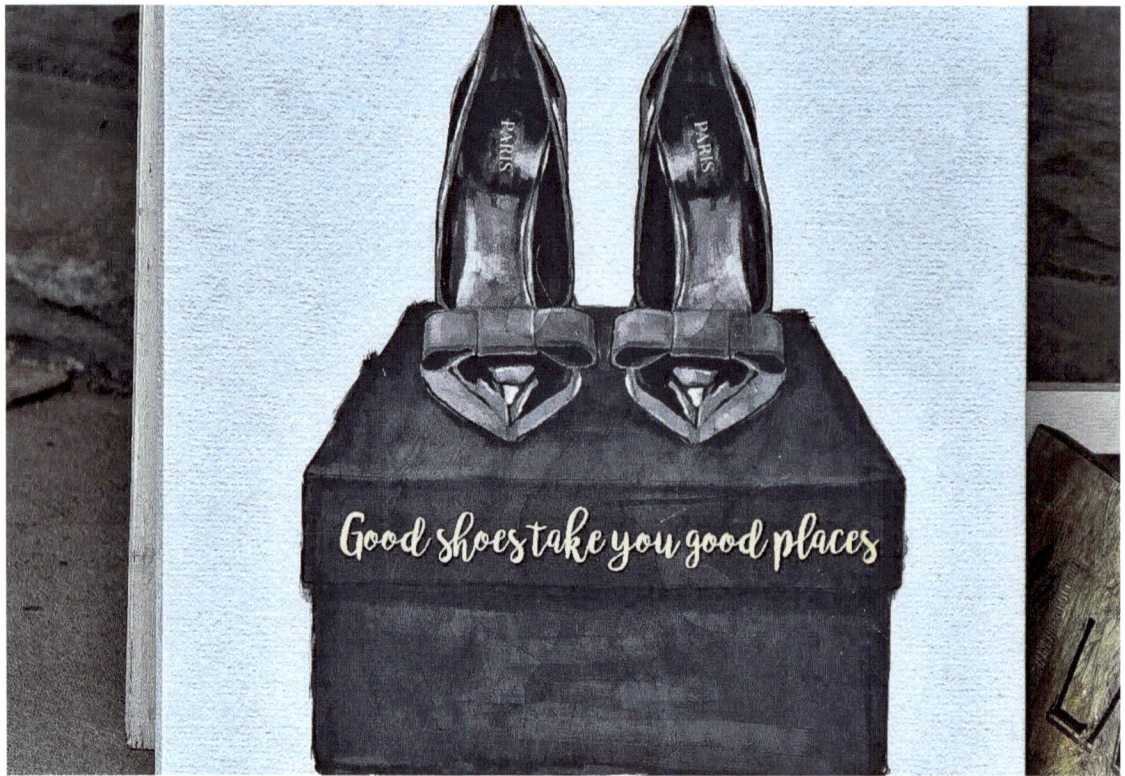

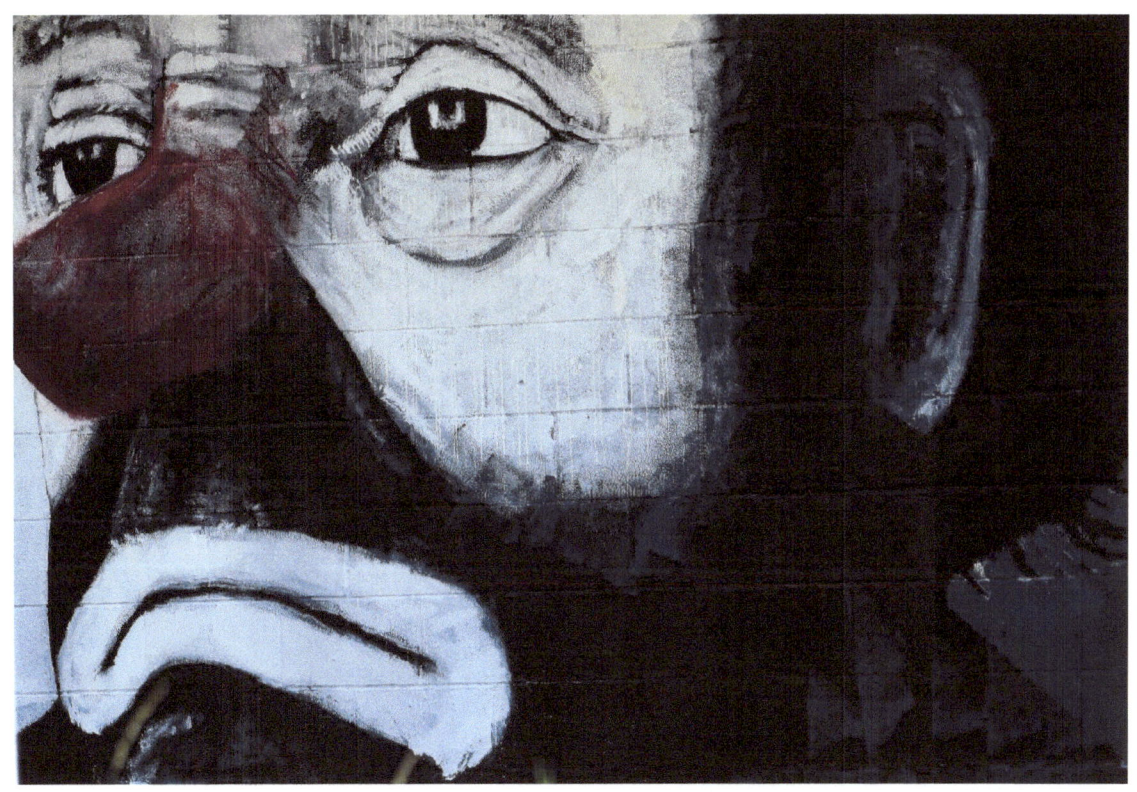
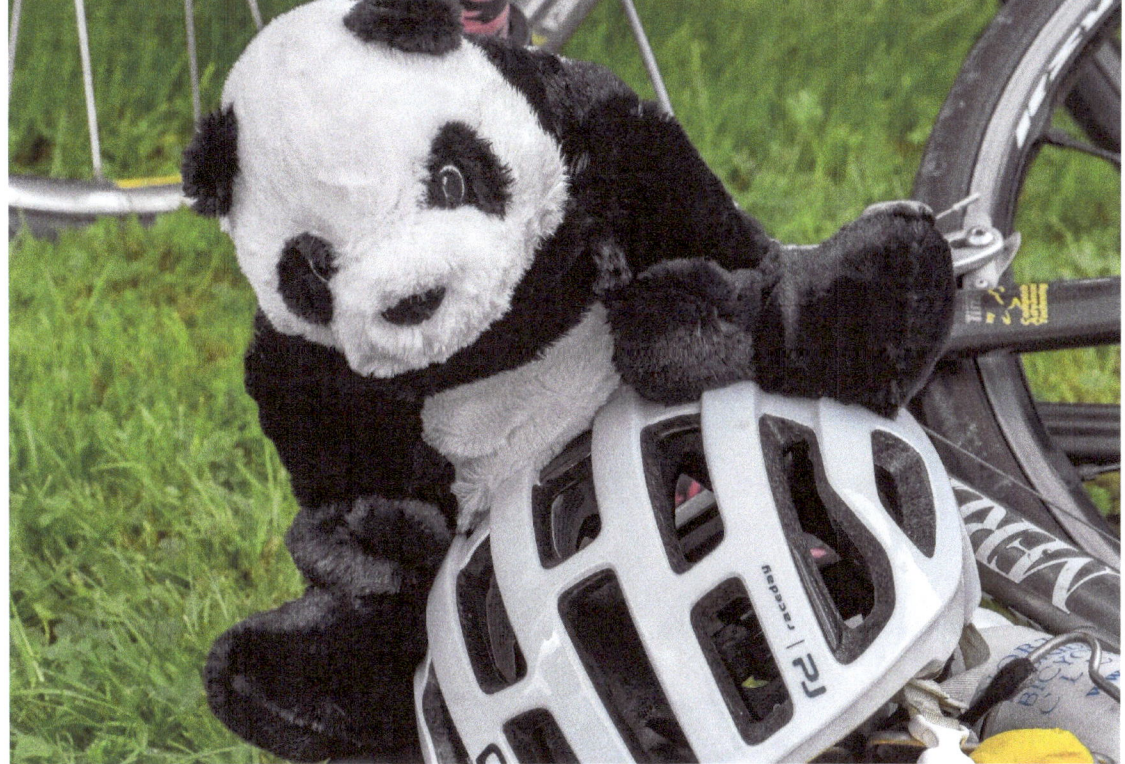

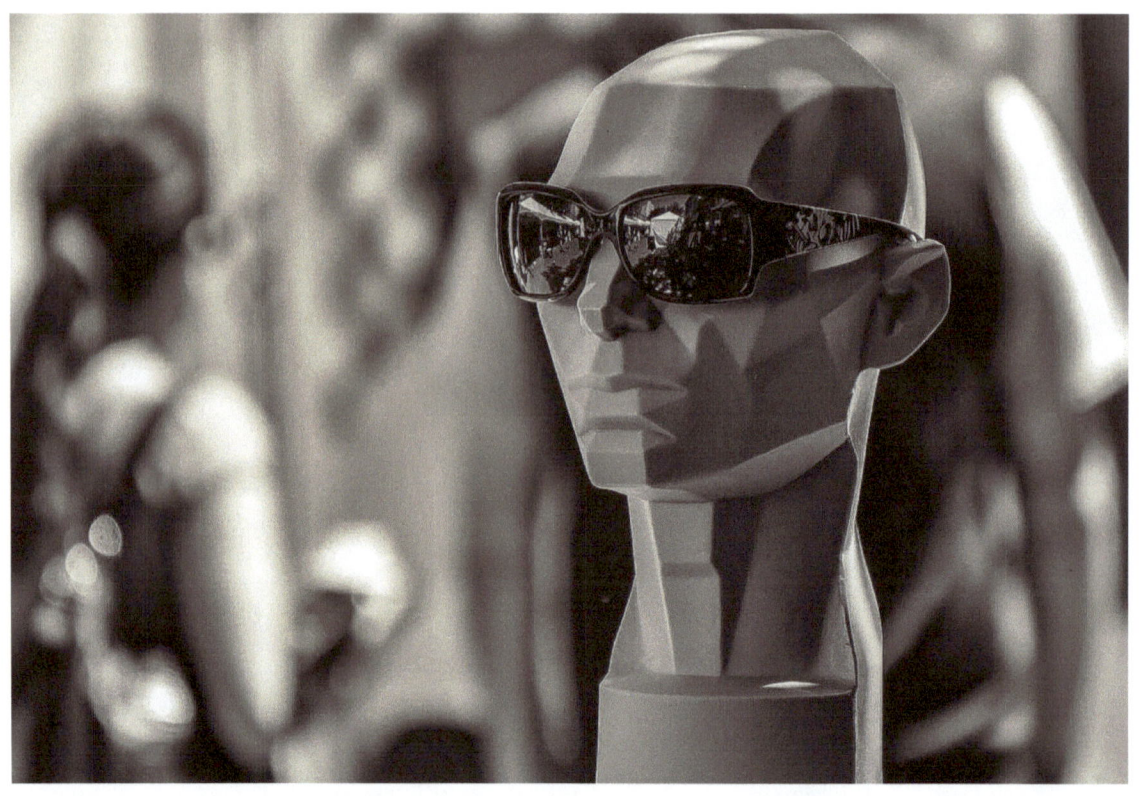
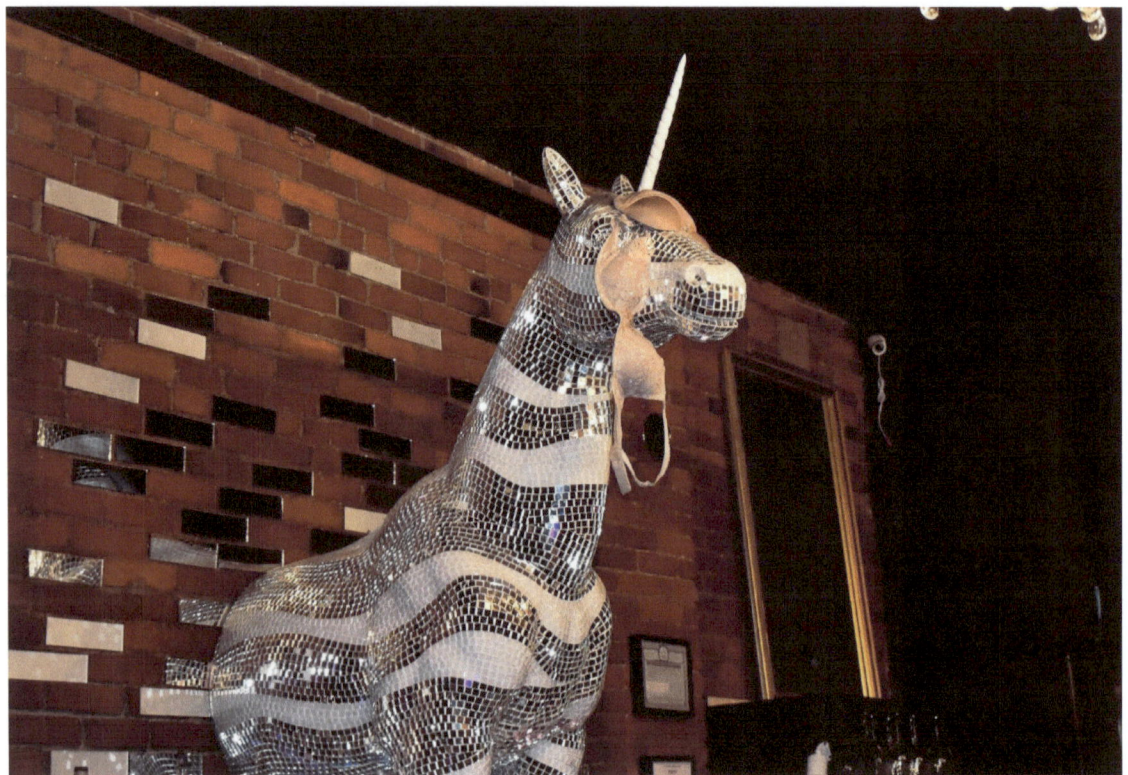

Furry, Feathery & In Between

Capturing images of our animal friends, especially our pets, and sharing them on social media has become a global pastime. If I am in the middle of a photoshoot and come across a dog basking in the sun, enjoying a belly rub or waiting for its human atop of sidewalk planter, I will quickly capture that memory.

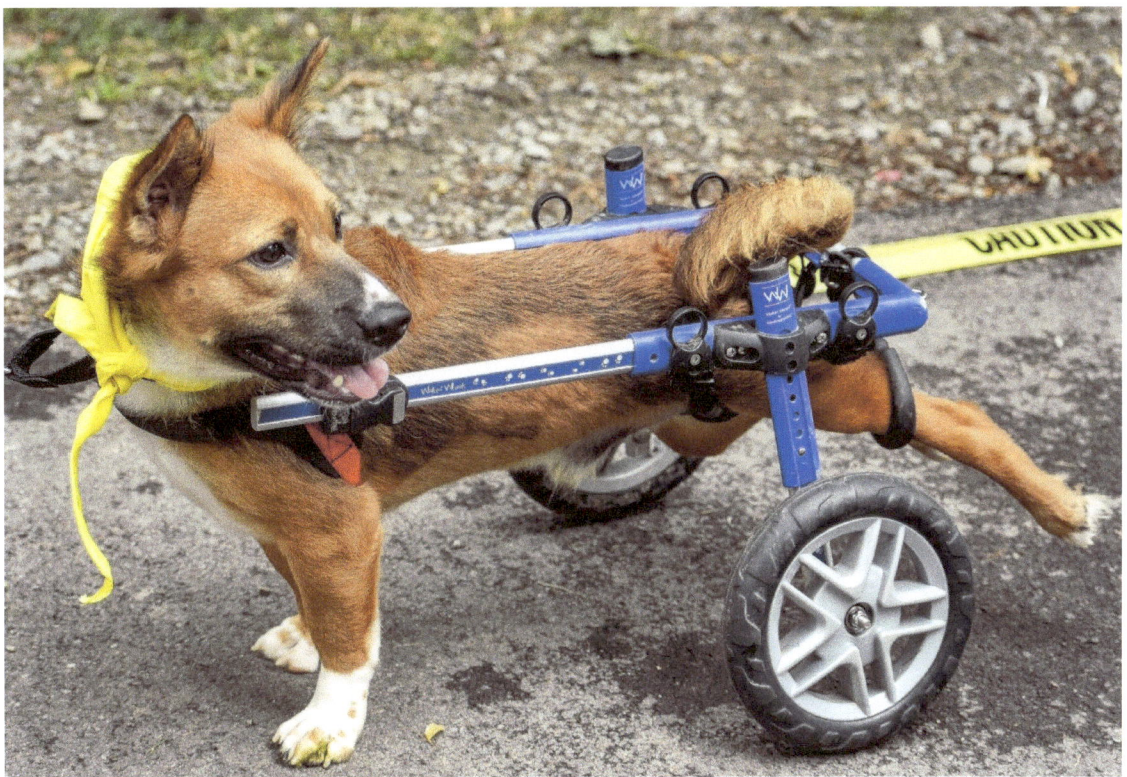

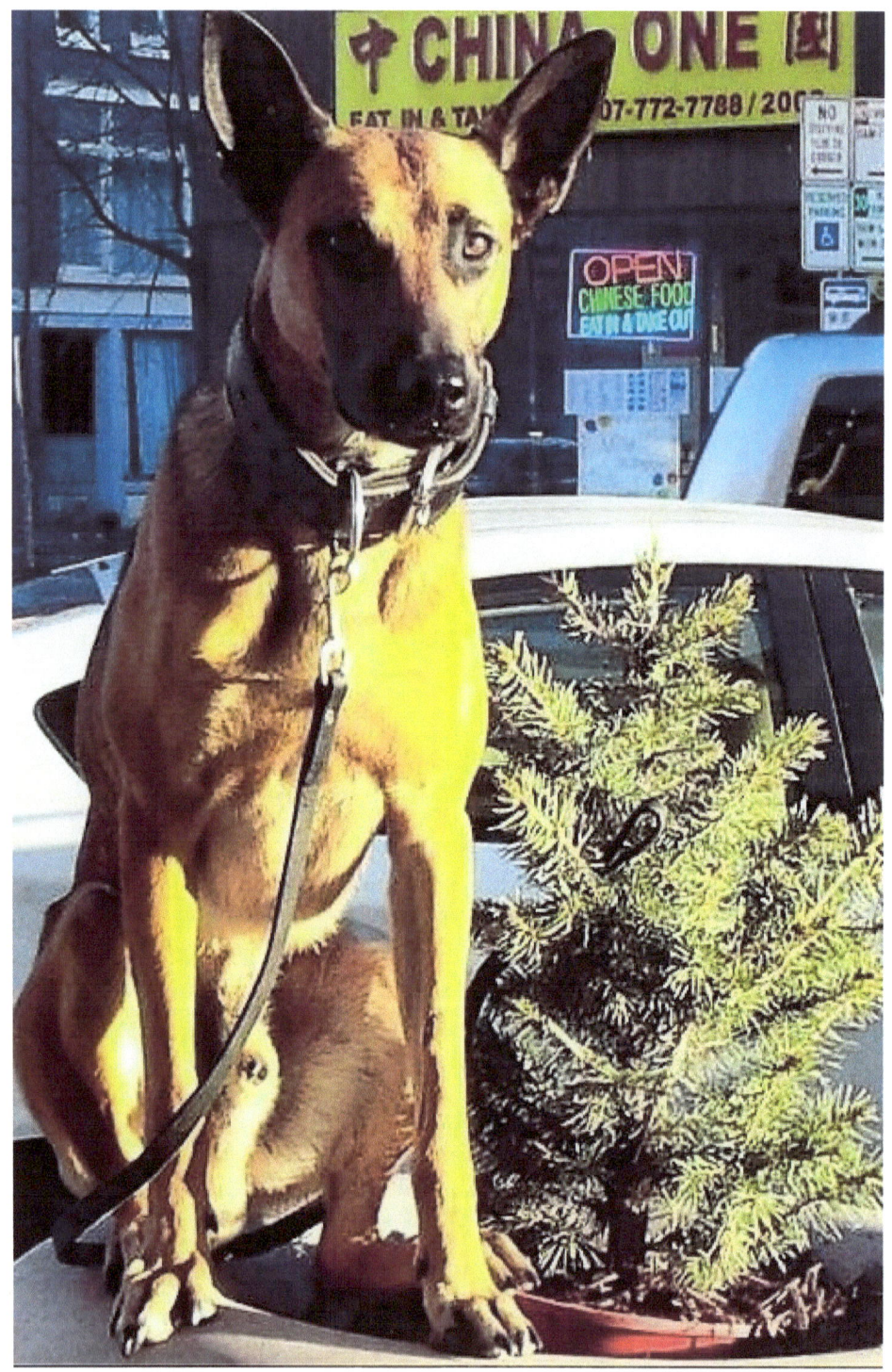

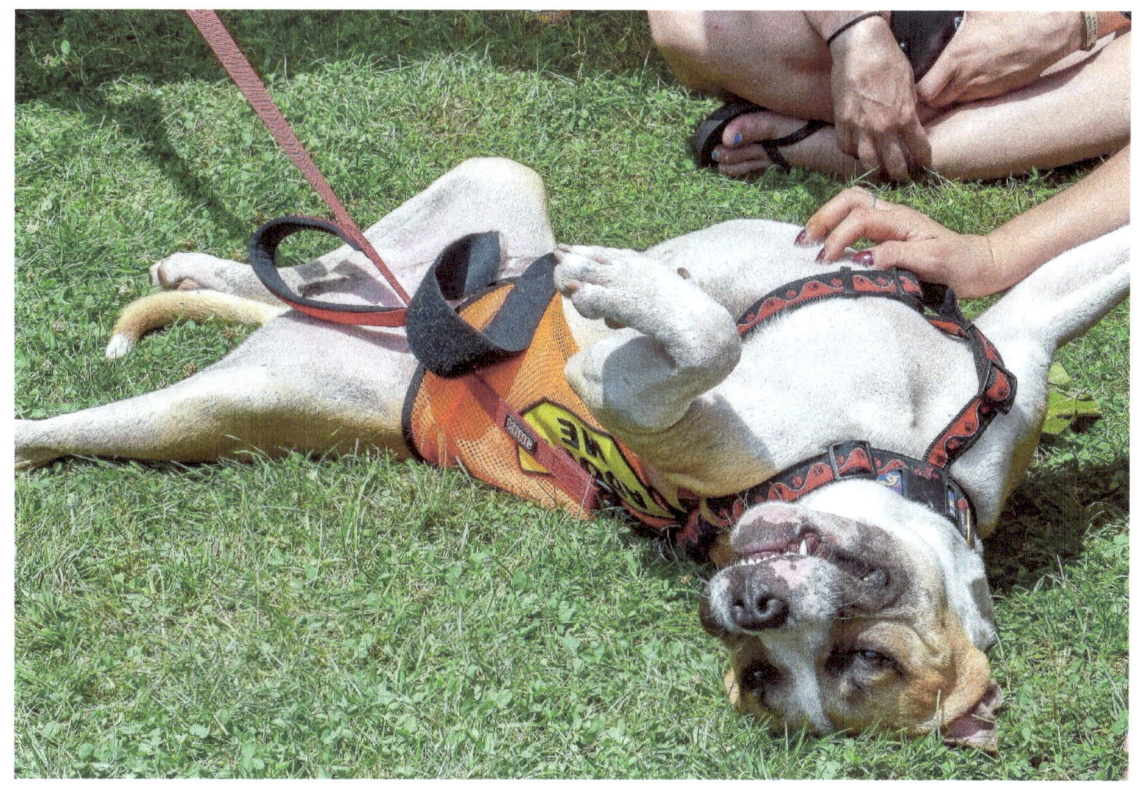

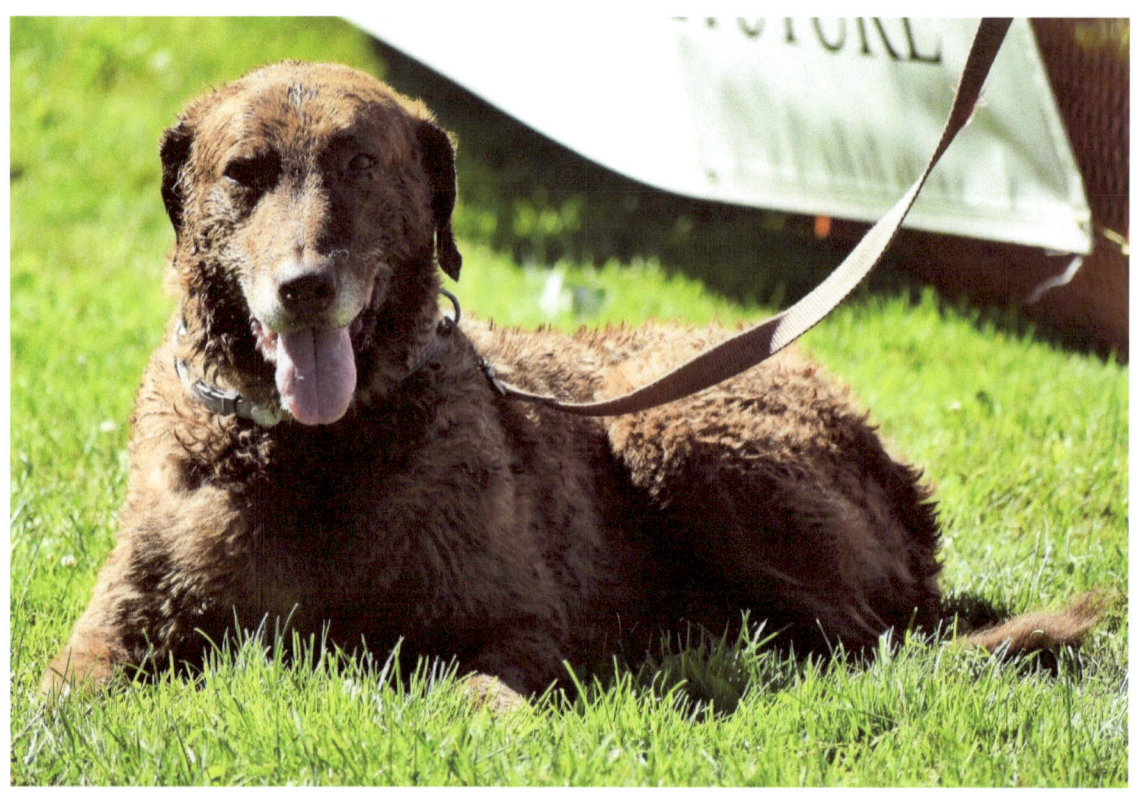
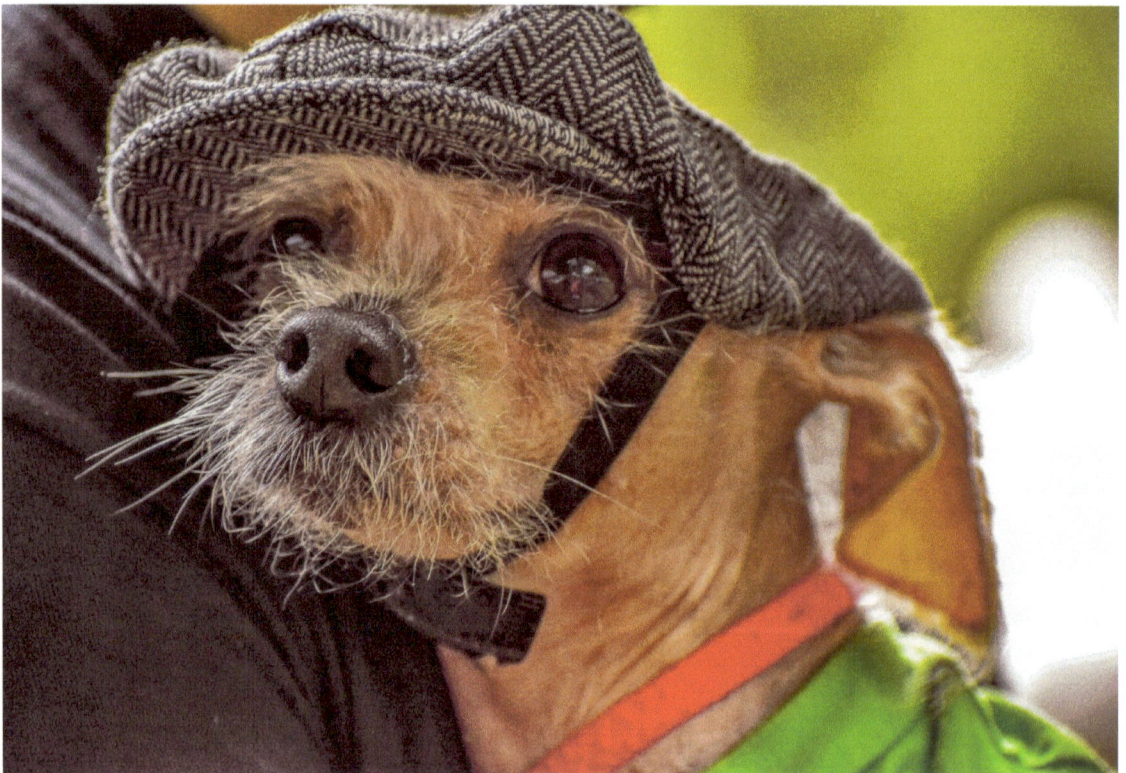

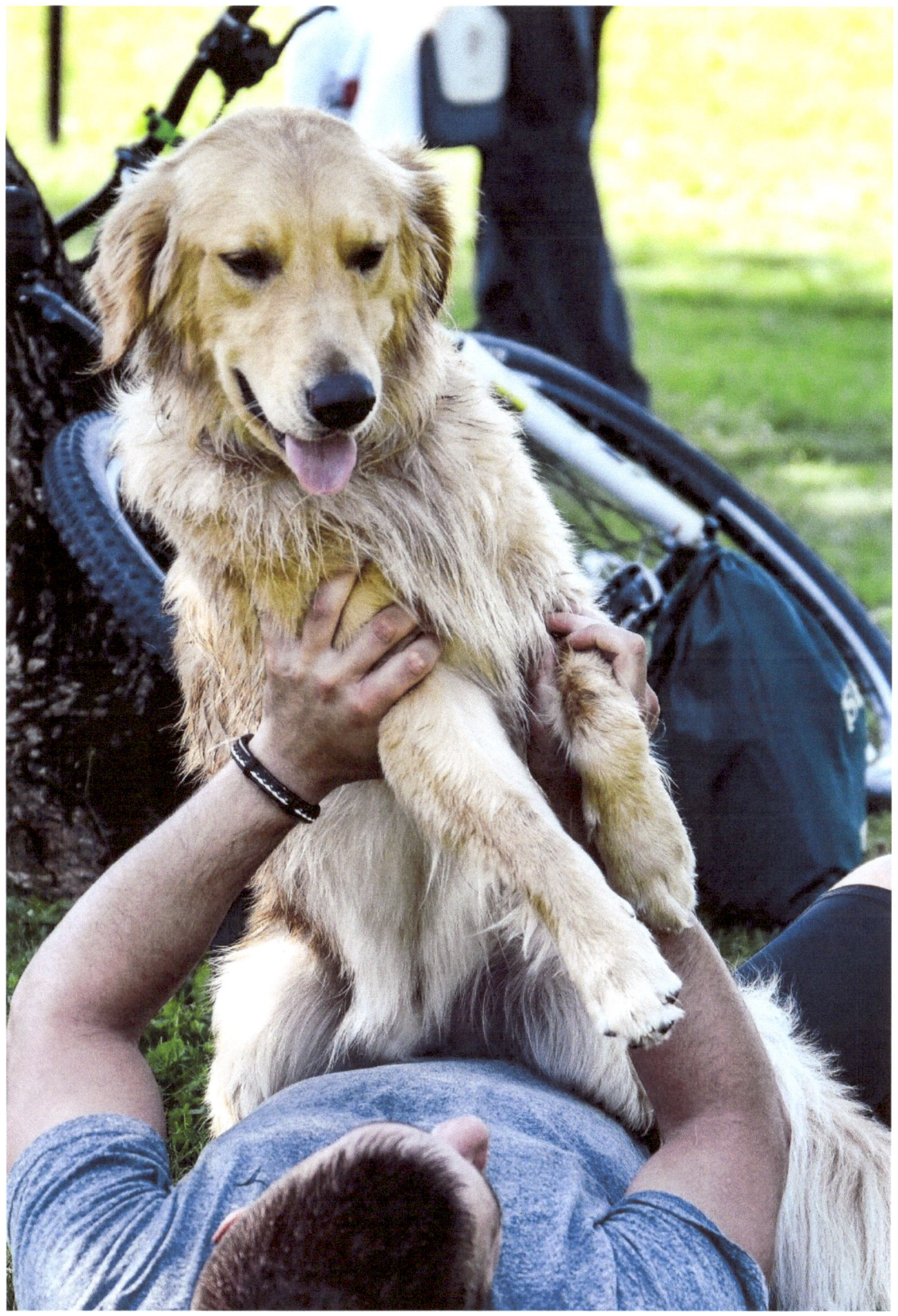

Of course, not all of my favorite animal shots are focused on man's best friend; nor are they all entirely focused on the furry. The feathery and scaley are also represented.

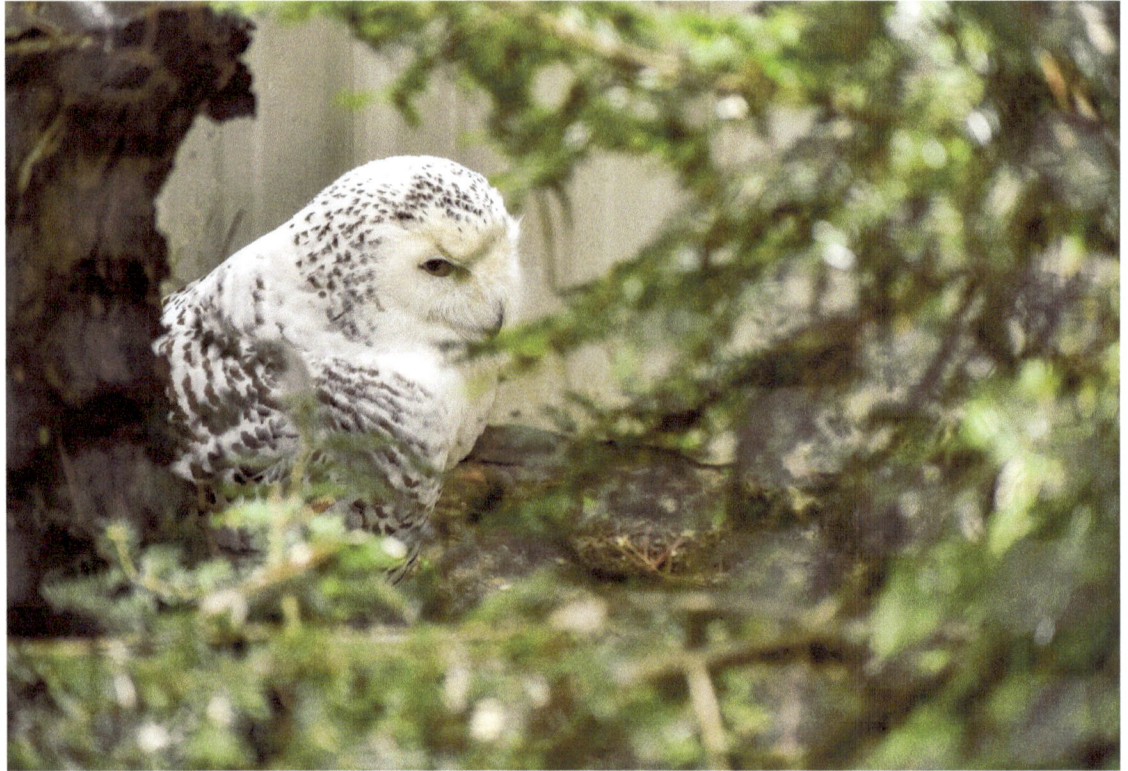

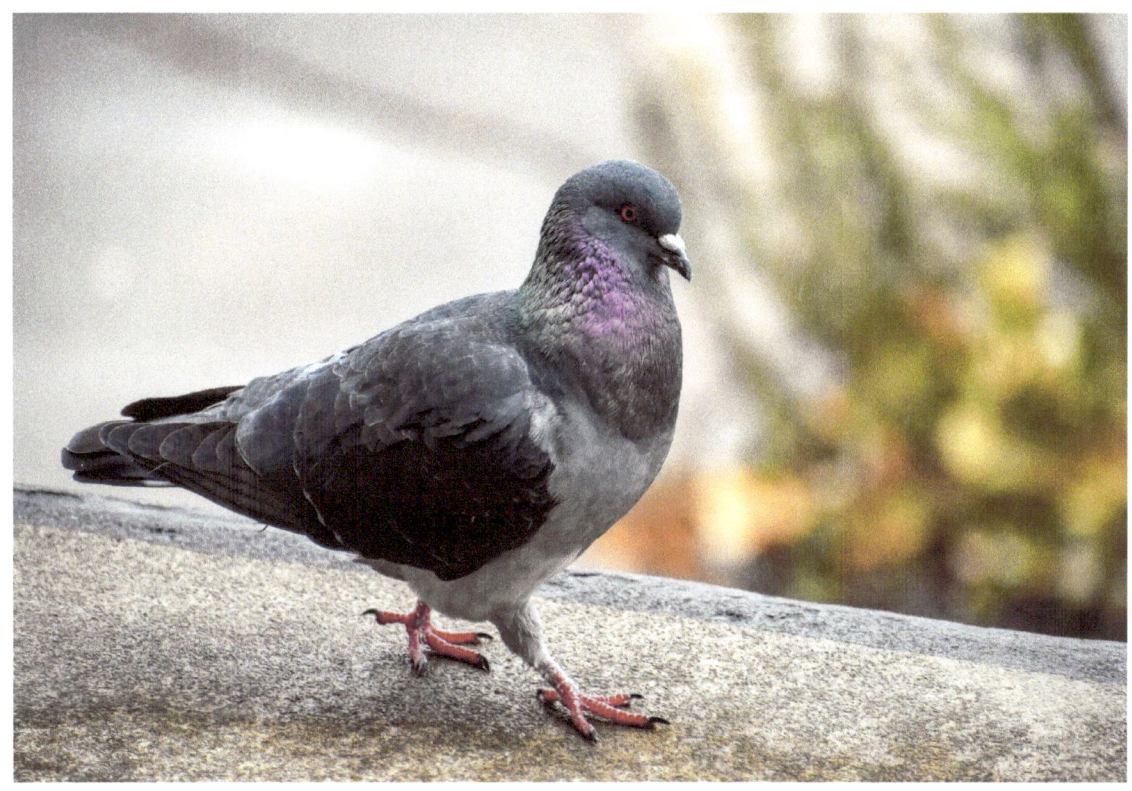
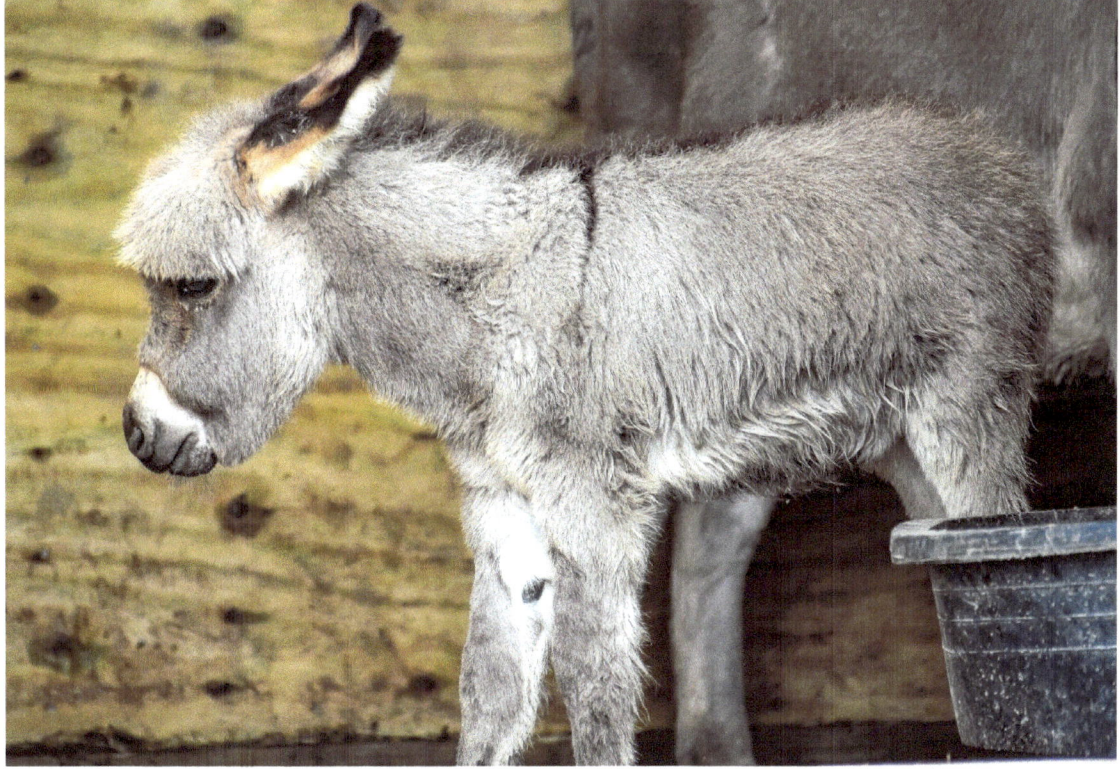

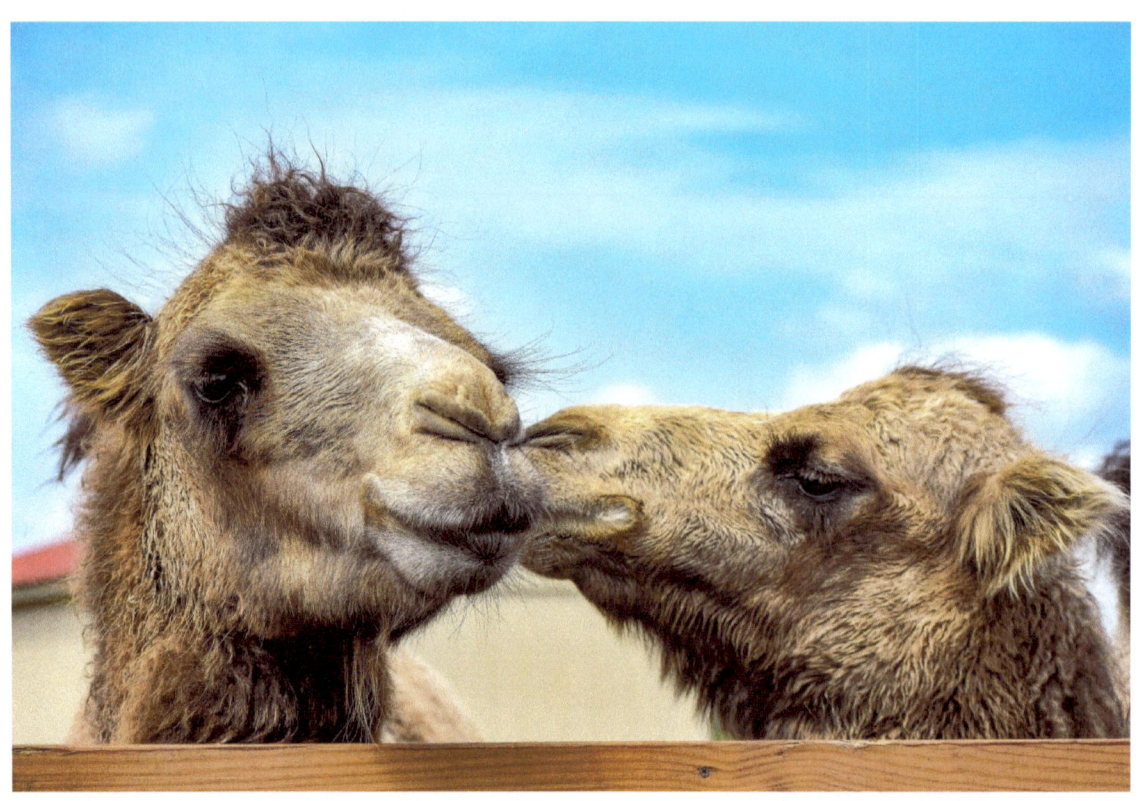
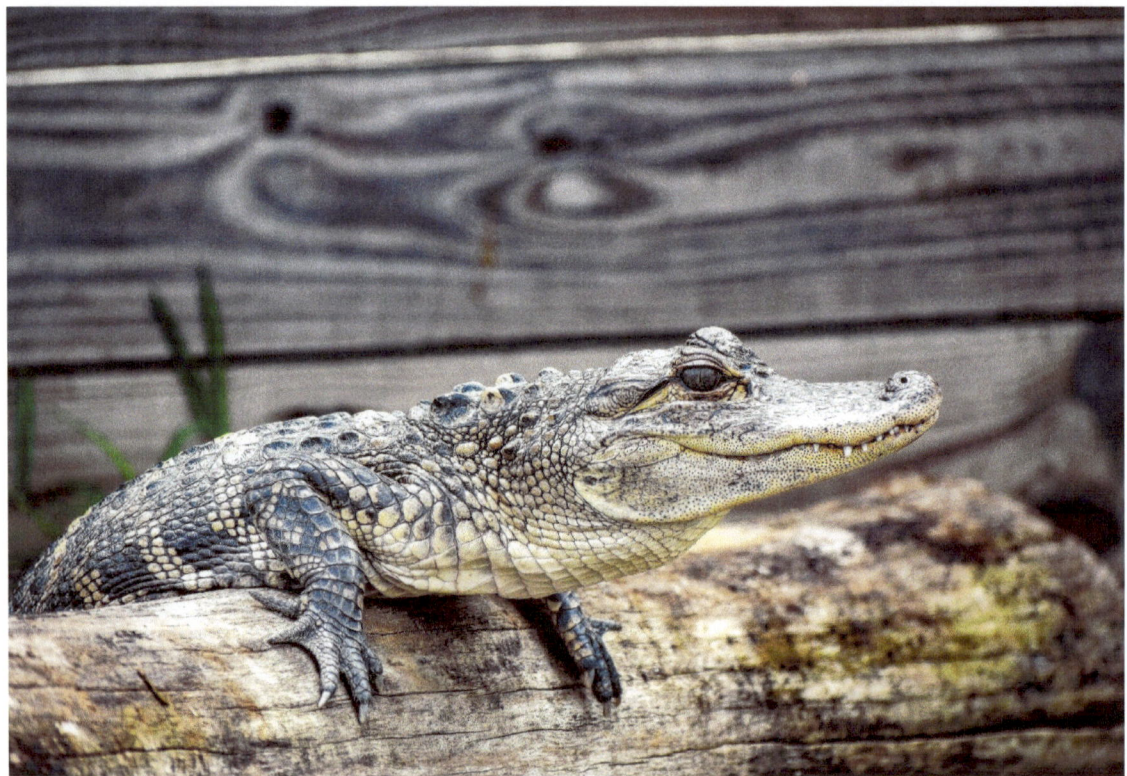

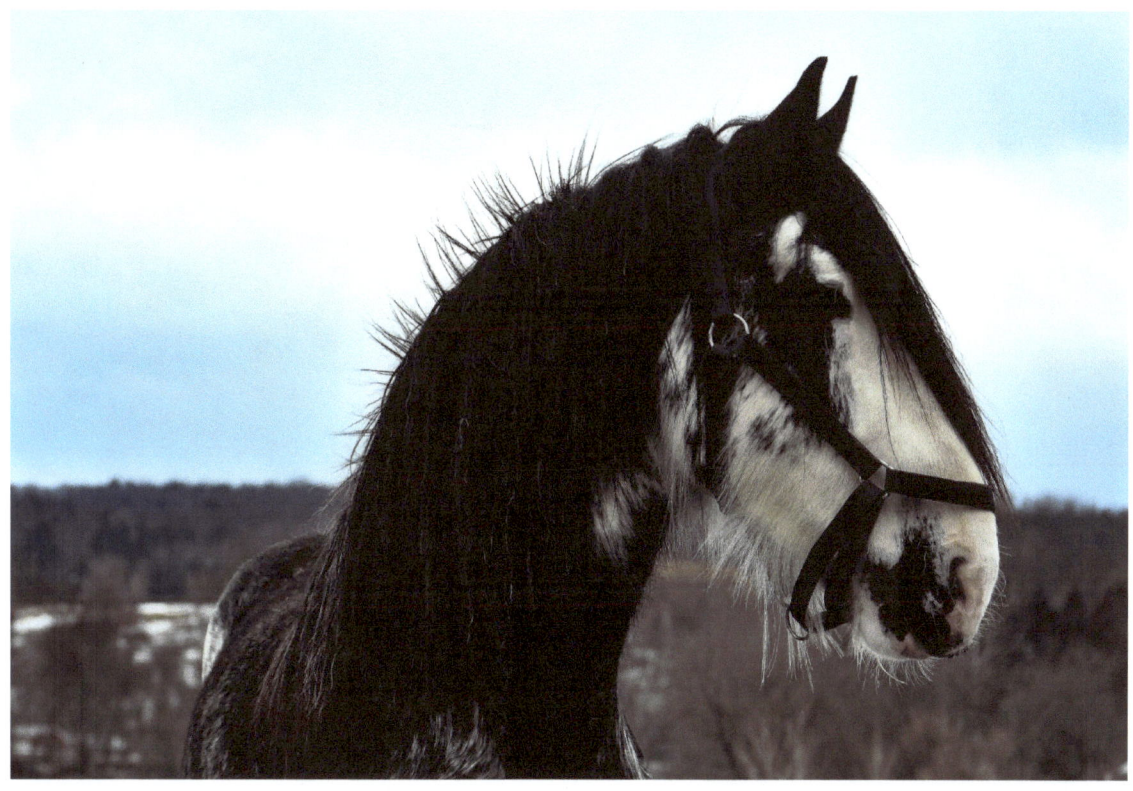
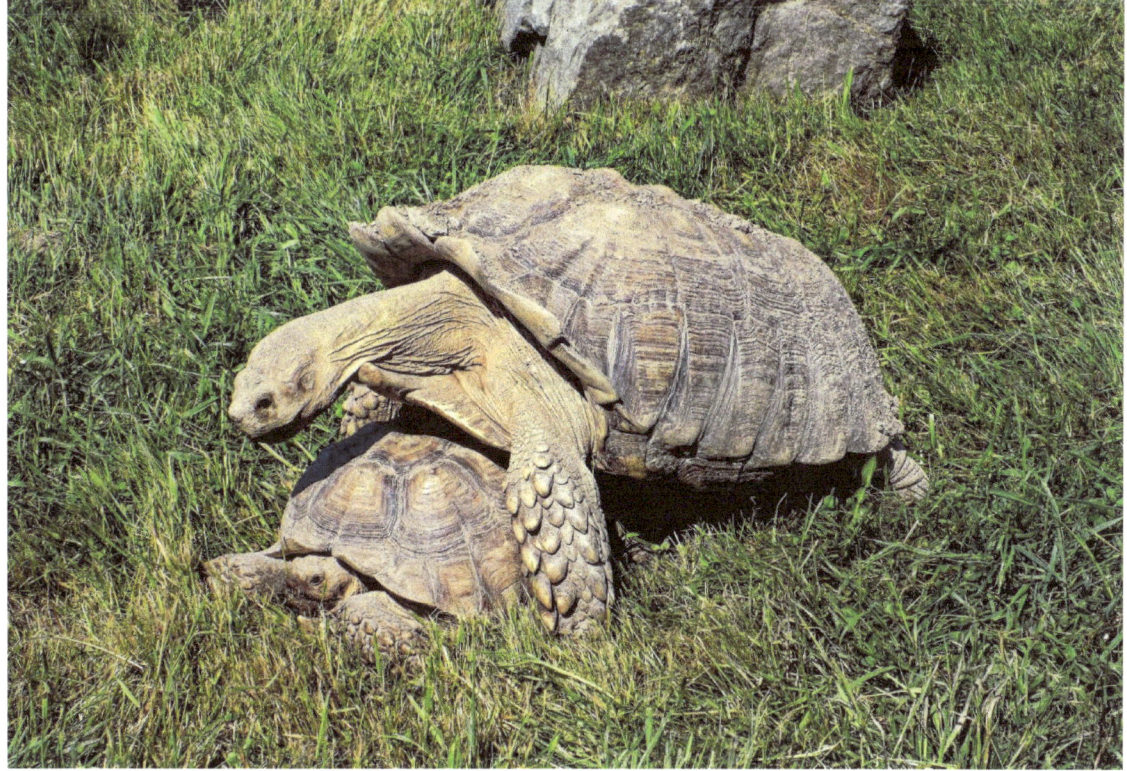

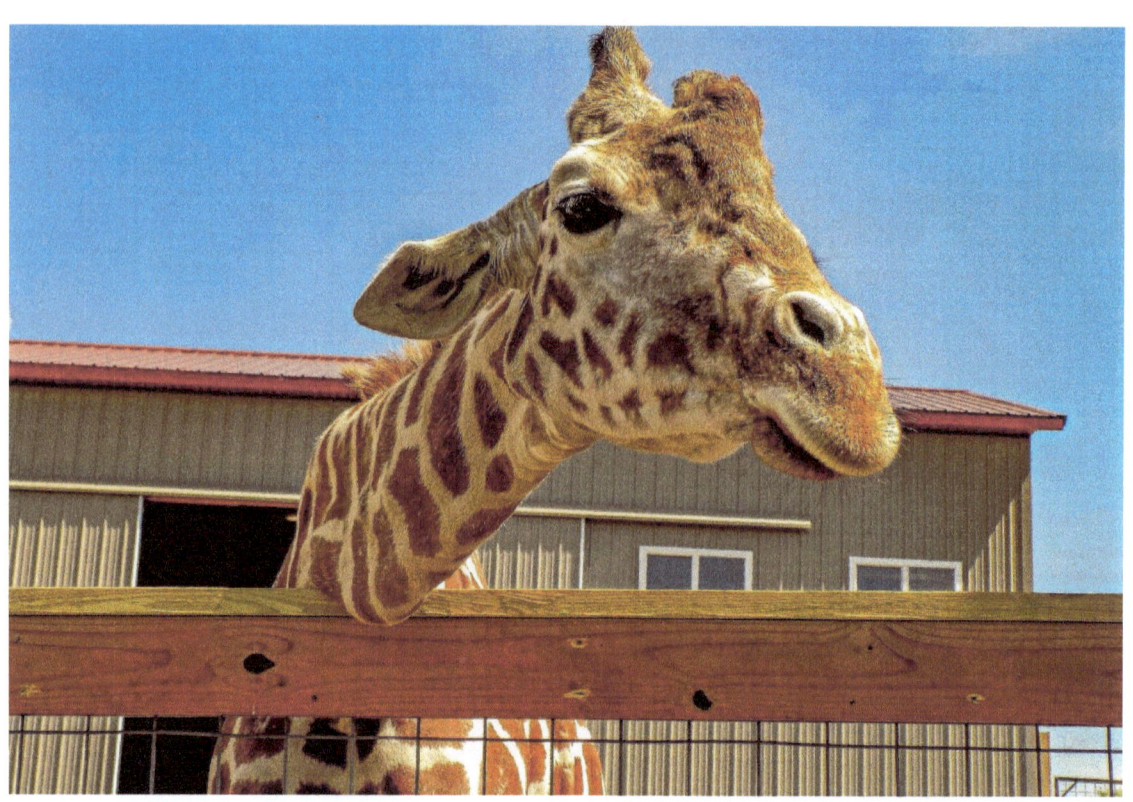
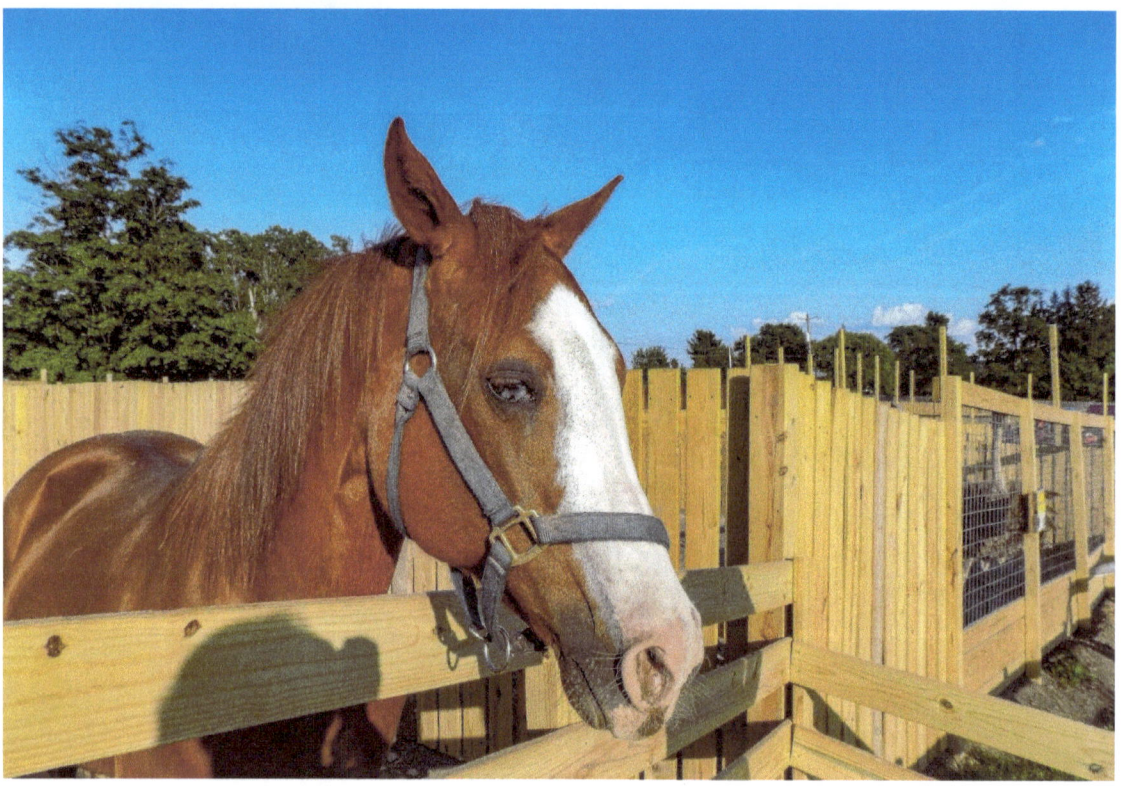

Floral Beauty

One could blame it on the gray, snowy northeast winters or simply on the exquisite beauty they reflect, but I cannot think of ending this book without some of the floral beauty I have encountered over the years.

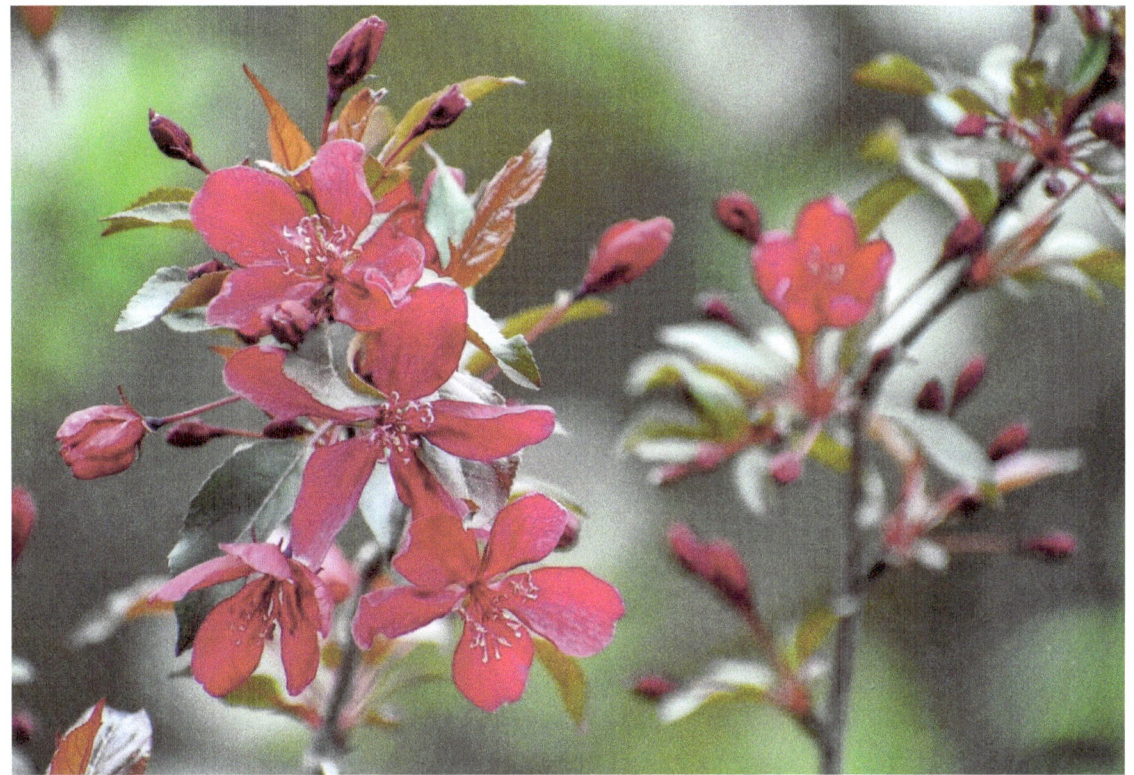

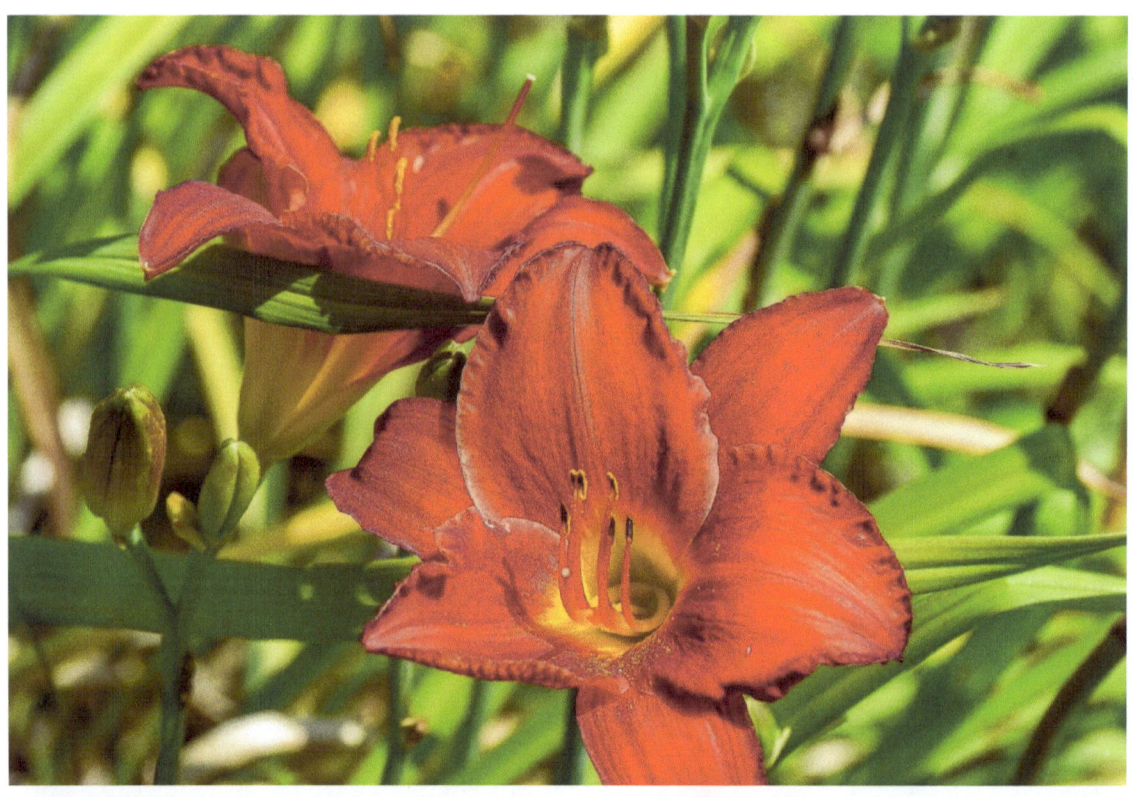
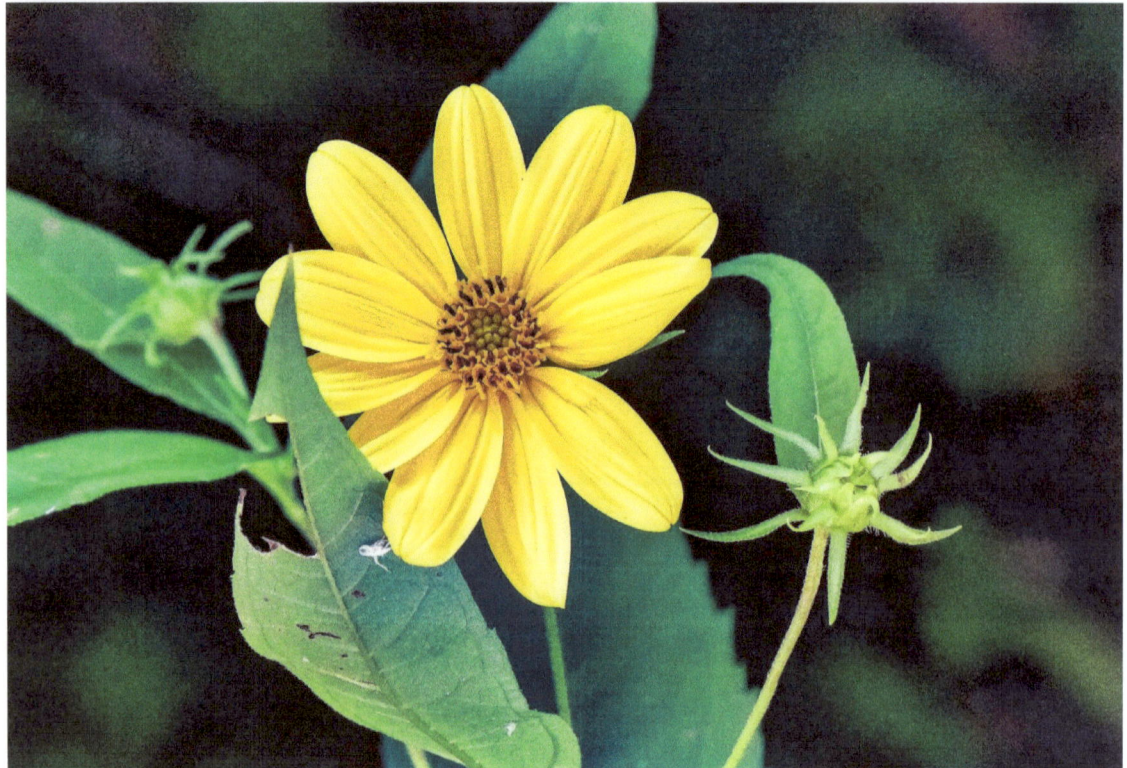

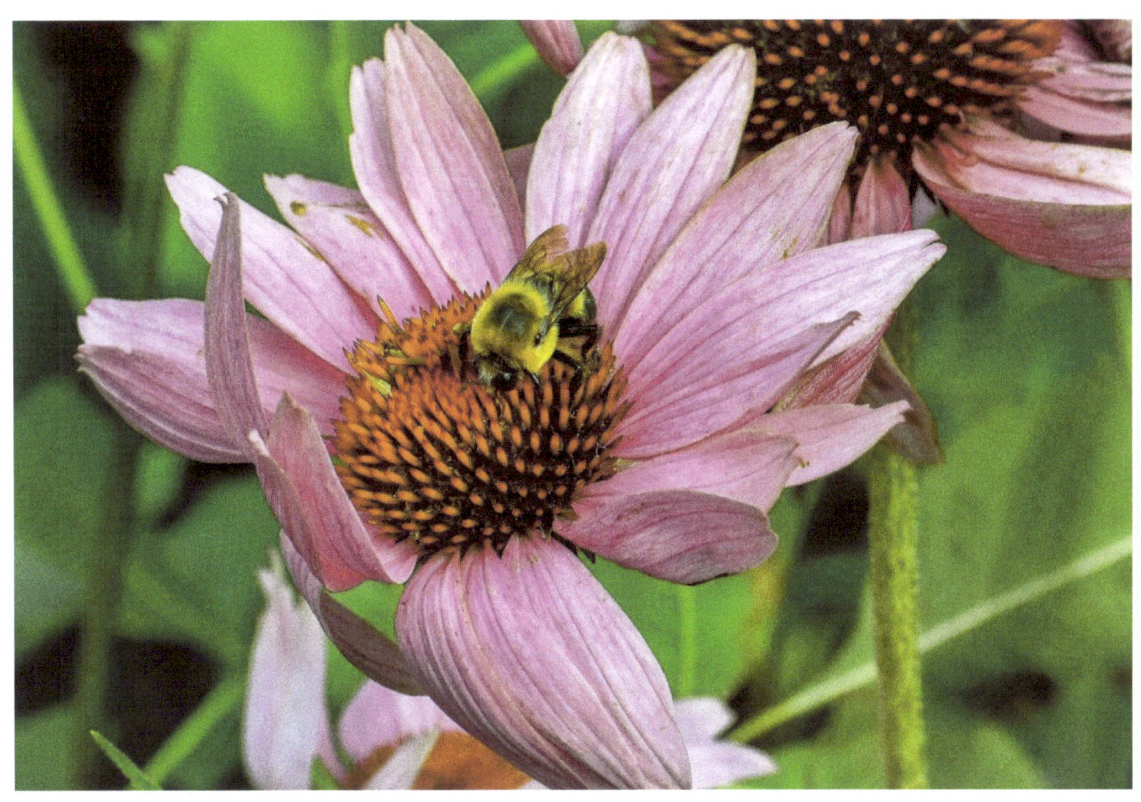

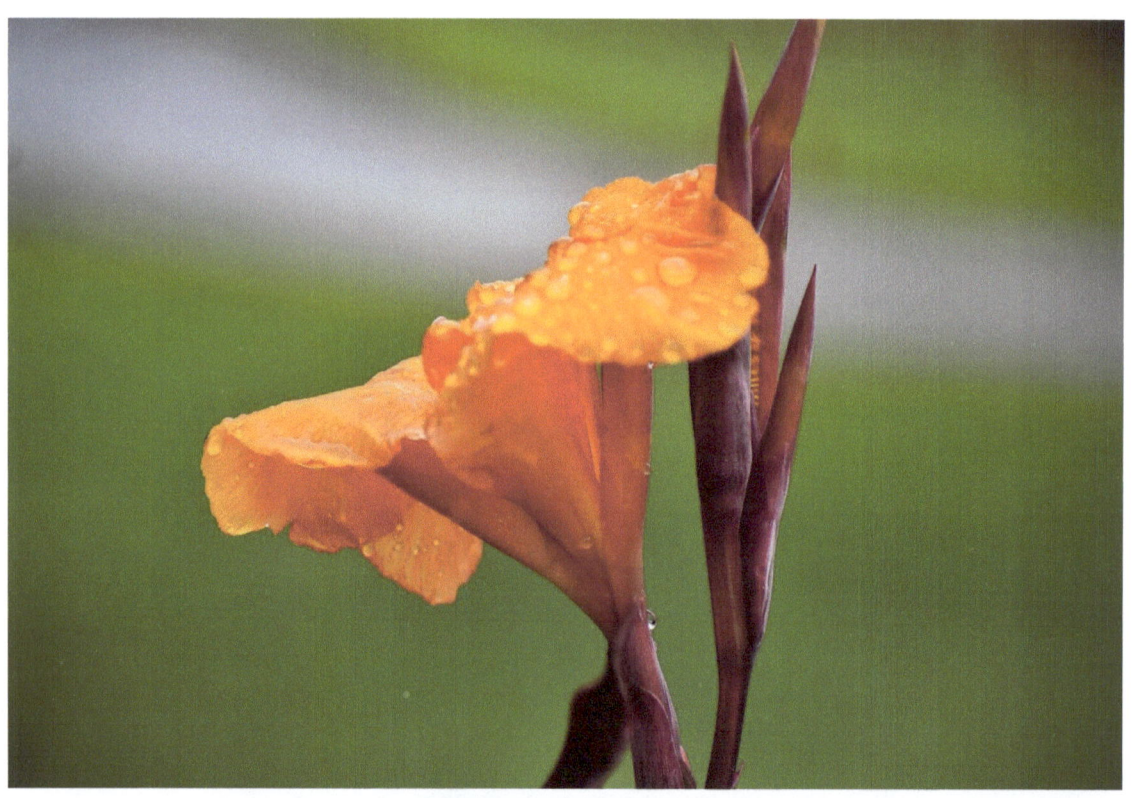
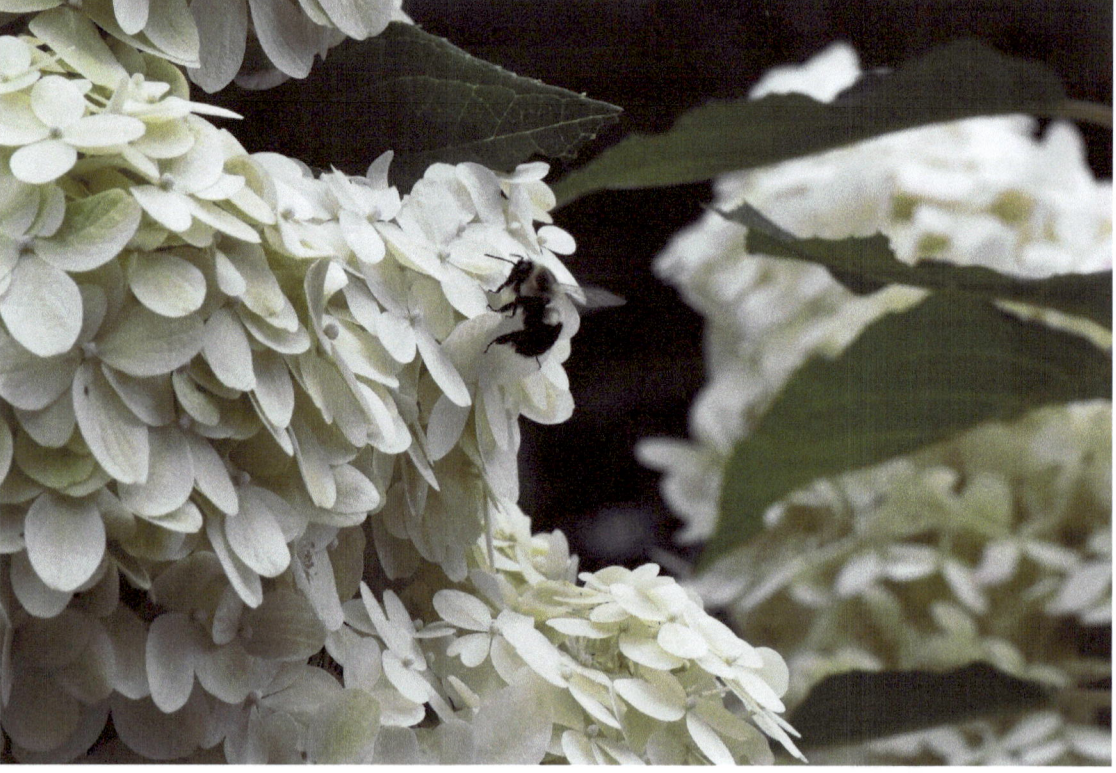

Conclusion

So that's it. My favorite people, places and things from the last six and a half years. Moving forward, I will continue to capture community memories while making more of my own. I encourage each and every one of you to capture your own memories; grab that cell phone or camera and go for it.

www.ingramcontent.com/pod-product-compliance
Lightning Source LLC
Chambersburg PA
CBHW051159220526
45473CB00003B/832